Advance Praise for *Turned On*

"A handbook for learning and unlearning our beliefs about people and business. You will either say, 'Finally, somebody said it!' or you will seriously question your assumptions about the path to success."
—*Rich Teerlink, president and CEO, Harley-Davidson, Inc.*

"Read *Turned On* for a behind-the-scenes look at how others are facing challenges similar to yours. Tear out all the 'Insight to Action' checklists, discuss one at each weekly meeting, and immediately implement those that will improve your business."
—*Tom Stemberg, chairman and CEO, Staples, Inc.*

"Open *Turned On* to any page and you will find a solid idea to consider for your own organization."
—*Richard G. LeFauve, chairman, Saturn Corporation*

"Dow and Cook draw the blueprint on how to unleash the full potential of everyone and realize their maximum potential contribution—and the backup examples are compelling. Wonderful lessons captured by two caring people."
—*Tom Malone, president and COO, Milliken Company*

"The leadership Insights are applicable in health care, business, the public sector, inner-city communities, or volunteer organizations. Dow and Cook clearly show the power of shared vision, values, and wisdom in achieving success."
—*Kathryn Johnson, president and CEO, The Healthcare Forum*

"*Turned On* clearly demonstrates how to build an organization where inspired employees take ownership of customer loyalty and financial results."
—*Leonard L. Berry, JCPenney Chair in Retailing Studies, Texas A&M University, and author of Leonard L. Berry on Great Service*

"Dow and Cook have essential wisdom and wonderful stories to share. *Turned On* is a must-have guide for any business trying to create a new tomorrow."
—*Wayne Huizenga, chairman, Huizenga Holdings, Inc.*

Turned On

Turned On

Eight Vital Insights to Energize Your People, Customers, and Profits

**ROGER DOW &
SUSAN COOK**

HarperBusiness
A Division of HarperCollinsPublishers

A hardcover edition of this book was published in 1996 by HarperBusiness, a division of HarperCollins Publishers.

HarperCollins books may be purchased for educational, business, or sales promotional use. For information please write: Special Markets Department, HarperCollins Publishers, Inc., 10 East 53rd Street, New York, NY 10022.

First paperback edition published 1997.

Designed by Irving Perkins Associates, Inc.

The Library of Congress has catalogued the hardcover edition as follows:

Dow, Roger J., 1946–
    Turned on : eight vital insights to energize your people, customers, and profits / Roger Dow & Susan Cook. — 1st ed.
      p. cm.
    Includes index.
    ISBN 0-88730-766-3
    1. Success in business.   2. Customer services.   3. Employee motivation.   I. Cook, Susan P., 1947–   .   II. Title.
    HF5386.D676   1996
    650.1—dc20   96-24998

ISBN 0-88730-861-9 (pbk.)

00 01 ❖/RRD 10

To Linda, Devon, and Blake with love and gratitude for understanding when the project took time away from us and, most of all, for your support and encouragement along the way.

ROGER

With heartfelt appreciation for my dear friends and family who believed in the possibilities of this book and endured my ongoing absences with humor, patience, and creativity.

SUE

Contents

Contents

Contents

Foreword

The essence of this superb book is captured in its two-word title, *Turned On*. You can have the world's greatest product backed up by the most magnificent business plan . . . but if your people (from the telephone operator to the CEO) aren't turned on . . . and your customers aren't *turned on* . . . forget it. It's all over . . . *period*.

In these crazy times, it's almost tragic to observe the "average" company, a multibillion-dollar global enterprise or the neighborhood hardware store, trying to succeed by delivering its product or providing service "a little bit faster or better" than yesterday or its competitor.

But . . . my wise friends Roger Dow and Sue Cook provide an in-depth look at exciting/enterprising/highly successful organizations that have found ways to break free of suffocating incrementalism to achieve truly stunning results. But (thankfully!) they don't take us on a forgettable tour of the "100 best companies at . . . whatever." Instead, they've kept it to a very memorable few extraordinary companies and let us learn about their bold and clever approaches directly from the people—not just the CEOs (which is fine), but (more important) from the front-line folks who are the ones who actually do turn on the customer and make the bottom line sparkle.

I believe what makes these companies stand out from

the growing crowd of look-alikes is their *obsession* with seeking their customers' *affection* . . . their unwillingness to be content with customer satisfaction. They are constantly looking for ways to *surprise* . . . not just please. They understand that customers are mostly influenced by the way they are handled moment-to-moment, and they urge their people to do whatever it takes to WOW their customers. They have developed a passionate, locally oriented service-delivery culture that is built on relationships developed one person at a time.

Roger and Sue also step outside the traditional business world to show what's possible when the folks at two atypical hospitals make a commitment to care more about the patients than is "permitted" by the ludicrous bureaucracy that is strangling health care today. It's exciting and at the same time depressing—why are these two exceptional hospitals able to turn on their teams to provide care and healing as any rational human being would want it, while the experience at too many other institutions is *de*humanizing, *de*moralizing, and downright *de*meaning?

I guess I'm most excited and encouraged by the awesome results the residents of the two inner-city communities highlighted in this book are achieving. They have literally succeeded on their own where politicians, government agencies, and well-intentioned assistance programs have failed miserably. And (hard to believe) I doubt there's a college degree, let alone an Ivy League MBA . . . or in most cases a high school diploma . . . hanging on the living-room walls of the participants. Yet these people have brilliantly used their instinctive wisdom, old-fashioned neighborhood pride, and sheer courage and determination to reclaim their home turf.

Turned On is required reading for anyone (hopefully that's all of us) who is concerned about the future of health care and our communities. These stunning examples of the profound power of relationships, caring, and individual responsibility should prompt any *Fortune* 500 company that is timid about letting its employees take charge and "own" their jobs to reconsider.

My only fear is that Roger and Sue have let these "real" people tell their wonderful stories (don't miss Charles the room-service waiter!) in such a colorful and engaging way. I frankly worry that the captivating stories may distract from the power in understanding and applying their systematically derived Eight Insights. They resist (praise be!) the temptation to state each Insight in some cute and catchy wording. Instead, they say it in clear, simple, plain English; e.g., Insight 4 is "Simplify, Simplify, Simplify." The language is simple, but the message is anything but simple-minded.

Turned On is straightforward and practical—nothing short of an implementable, full-blown business plan for your enterprise (whether you're a three-person start-up or you're looking to inject some life, excitement, and vibrance into a mature organization).

The question I am most frequently asked is, "How can we implement this stuff?" Well, Roger and Sue have not left us dangling. I found the "Insight to Action" recommendations to be solid, applicable, and an excellent way to increase your capabilities in any given area.

Roger Dow and Sue Cook have put together a compelling road map on how to achieve the payoffs and possibilities that result from "turned on" people . . . and customers. I can't imagine how anyone trying to make a meaningful difference in business, the public sector, or their community would not benefit from this book. It is filled with leadership lessons everyone can profit from. So . . . get started . . . *and* have fun along the way!

Tom Peters
Coauthor of In Search of Excellence

[Michelangelo's] *first lesson had been that the power and the durability lay in the stone, not in the arms or tools. The stone was master; not the mason. If ever a mason came to think he was master, the stone would oppose and thwart him. And if a mason beat his stone as an ignorant* contadino *might beat his beasts, the rich, warm, glowing, breathing material became dull, color-less, ugly; died under his hand . . . To sympathy, it yielded; grew even more luminous and sparkling, achieved fluid forms and symmetry.*

Stone works with you. It reveals itself. Its nature is to change. Each stone has its own char-acter. It must be understood. Handle it carefully, or it will shatter. Never let the stone destroy itself. Stone gives itself to skill and love.

Stone will speak to you. Listen . . .

—IRVING STONE
The Agony and the Ecstasy

Long-Term Vitality

Looking at their somber faces, my gut confirmed that the rumors were true. It was November of 1990 and Bill Marriott had gathered our senior management team—colleagues and friends I'd grown up with since joining Marriott in college as a lifeguard at our sixth hotel.

"I'm not going to lie to you," were Bill's opening words. "We have very serious problems. We can make payroll through April, maybe May. We've built a wonderful organization together—it's more like a family than a business. Our 209,000 associates are counting on us, and we can't let them and their families down. It won't be easy, but I'm confident we can turn this thing around . . . "

Wall Street didn't share Bill's optimism and our stock dove to 8⅜—thirty-four points from its high three years before. I spoke about our dilemma with Sue Cook, president of Think Customer, who consults and coaches senior managers on how to build a customer-driven organization. Most of her assignments involve turnaround situations, and by the time she's called in it's pretty desperate.

It was hard to believe what Roger was telling me, but I'd seen too many companies go down the same road. They were the darlings of their industries who could do no wrong—and suddenly the market, the economy, or a competitor changed the rules, pulling the rug out from under them. The warning signs are always there, but tough to notice when you're doing so well. Sometimes the eyes of an outsider can see most clearly.

We had an idea. Let's bring together leaders from a wide variety of thriving businesses to share their real-world experiences. If we could assemble such a group, it would be an opportunity to learn and grow from fresh perspectives. Would Bill Marriott be willing to host such a gathering?

I discussed our idea with Bill. "I don't think the timing is right," he said. "With all our problems, who are we to be telling people what they should be doing?" Bill said he would attend if we clearly positioned it as an informal occasion to listen to one another and share what works and, more important, what doesn't.

Sixty days later twenty-four CEOs and senior executives from highly profitable, values-driven organizations descended on Marriott's Camelback Inn Resort. Many were from America's most admired public companies such as AT&T, Charles Schwab, Intel, Merck, and Pepsi-Cola Company. Others represented highly respected private organizations like Mary Kay Cosmetics, Milliken, RE/MAX, and Sewell Motor Company.

For two days leaders candidly described what drove their successes and where they had stumbled. Mark Scott, CEO of Mid-Columbia Medical Center, electrified the group with his simple reminder: "We're talking about people here—our sons and daughters, mothers and fathers, husbands and wives—not a bunch of faceless statistics. We've got to restore the respect, dignity, and passion within each of us."

On the final night the group sat around a campfire atop Mummy Mountain sharing the hopes, dreams, and aspirations we had for our organizations. "Roger, you and Sue have pulled together an extraordinary group," marveled Bill Marriott. "Listening to these people verifies what we have to do. We've been too worried about ten-year plans and strategies. We need to get back to the roots of our culture, get closer than ever to our people and our customers."

OUR LEARNING COLLABORATIVE

That was five years ago, and our learning collaborative—the **Service/Quality Leadership Forum 2000**—has come together every six months since. Gatherings are now hosted by CEOs at their companies. We explore behind the scenes, talk to the people, and learn firsthand what fuels their greatness. Our forum now includes fifty organizations that contribute to an ever-growing abundance of exhilarating knowledge.

TURNED ON

Many leaders asked us to synthesize our five years of learning—passionate people, incredible stories, and real-world lessons—so they could teach and inspire their own people. The two of us began sifting through the wealth of knowledge, searching for themes and commonalities.

One factor is unmistakable: certain organizations operate at a higher energy level than others. People in these companies are inspired, passionate, and alive. Customers buzz about their latest experience. Profits soar. When people talk about these organizations, they use phrases like *on fire, exciting, passionate,* and *electrified*. We decided to find out what creates such palpable passion—the makings of a Turned On organization.

Organizations that are ablaze with success don't get there using a program of the month to generate excitement. Their synergy and dynamism spring from a deep commitment to *long-term vitality*. Turned On organizations strive to be vibrant, strong, and growing for decades to come.

Our investigations uncovered the "what" and "how" of long-term success. Vitality springs from balance—an equal obsession with energized people, enthusiastic customers, and financial performance.

Businesses today are often alarmingly out of balance—too many companies focus only on short-term financial results. The company may post phenomenal numbers for a few years, but these results are slowly undermined by employee apathy and customer indifference. Great organizations are relentless in their attention to the bottom line, but they balance that intensity with an equal emphasis on their people and customers.

But how does a company infuse balance into the fabric of the organization? From our learnings we distilled Eight Vital Insights that reveal how to achieve balance. These are the building blocks of long-term vitality and a Turned On organization:

Insight 1: Build a Strong Foundation

Insight 2: Make Every Customer Feel Special

Insight 3: Have the Courage to Set Bold Goals

Insight 4: Simplify, Simplify, Simplify

Insight 5: Make Technology Your Servant

Insight 6: Measure Well, Act Fast

Insight 7: Unleash the Power of People

Insight 8: Lead with Care

We played this back to the organizations of the **Service/Quality Leadership Forum 2000** and shared the Eight Insights with thousands of people during speeches and presentations. In every instance the message resonated strongly. We knew we'd tapped into something big—too big to keep to ourselves.

ENTHUSIASTIC CUSTOMERS

INSPIRED PEOPLE

FINANCIAL PERFORMANCE

8. Lead with Care

7. Unleash the Power of People

6. Measure Well, Act Fast

5. Make Technology Your Servant

4. Simplify, Simplify, Simplify

3. Have the Courage to Set Bold Goals

2. Make Every Customer Feel Special

1. Build a Strong Foundation

The Turned On Organization

To deepen our understanding and create this book, we personally visited a select few Turned On organizations. Their diversity in size, scope, and industry demonstrates the universal applicability of the Eight Insights. We've spent the last two years speaking not only with CEOs but with senior managers, line managers, frontline workers, and even customers. We present their compelling stories in their own words so you can learn directly from their wisdom.

Our book describes each of the Eight Insights and the practices used to achieve them. Each practice is supported by an "Insight to Action" checklist of real-world exercises to implement immediately.

At the end of the book is a "Vitality Scorecard." Use it to assess the balance of your organization today and to prioritize your action plan. *We strongly disagree with those who say you must throw everything out and start over with a clean slate.* Build on what's already working for you.

A Turned On organization maintains a balanced emphasis on people, customers, and profits and uses the Eight Insights to achieve growth and long-term vitality, as shown by this model.

Our Eight Insights are not theories—the companies featured in this book apply them relentlessly to achieve extraordinary results by any standard. Seven made *Fortune* magazine's 1996 list of America's Most Admired Companies. Three are Malcolm-Baldrige National Quality Award winners. Five years ago, if you bought one share of stock in each of our book's publicly traded companies, your investment would have increased 215 percent while the Standard

& Poor index increased only 17 percent. During that time their total revenue increased 300 percent, and their profits have gone up a whopping 600 percent.

You'll also meet community organizations that restore balance to achieve incredible success. We'll show you how two hospitals are reinventing the future of health care. You'll learn how a pair of inner-city communities reduced violent crime by 45 percent and cut the number of people on unemployment and welfare by 50 percent with no government support.

Each of these various organizations labels itself a "work in progress" and admits it doesn't have all the answers. But taken together as a whole, we think they do. They have one thing in common: they pursue long-term vitality guided by an equal obsession with energized people, enthusiastic customers, and financial performance. They are Turned On!

RESTORING BALANCE

The true face of long-term vitality might surprise you—*the future of business lies in the ability to use modern capabilities to recapture the personal relationships of times past*. When companies were smaller and less complex, there existed a healthy balance between making money and doing what was right for people and customers. Personal relationships, tailored products, and handcrafted service were the rule.

The desire to treat people like human beings—and to be

treated like a human being yourself—is human nature. But as organizations grew in size and complexity it became nearly impossible to offer a personal relationship. Companies struggled to emulate relationships with *standardized* policies and procedures to make their people deliver consistent service. Organizations were *personalized*—providing cranked-out "Have a nice day!" service.

The organizations in this book use modern capabilities to return full circle to *personal* products, services, and relationships. In striking a balance among people, customers, and profits, they rekindle a feeling of comfort and rightness that we all intuitively cherish. The chief of staff at Harbor Hospital, speaking about its cutting-edge, high-tech approach to patient-centered healing, remarked, "It reminds me of the way we cared for the sick back in my small village in India. The family is involved, the friends are involved, and the responsibility of care is shared by the whole community." A customer of USAA, the multibillion-dollar insurance and financial services company, told us, "They know me so well I feel like they're the local insurance man who lives around the corner and has known my family for years."

We intuitively know why a company is more successful when it taps into the human values of the past. Your organization accelerates to high speed when you throw out unnecessary manuals and policies and liberate your people to treat customers properly. People make the right decisions effortlessly and feel good about the work they do. Customers are not just satisfied, they are enthusiastic and tell everyone they know about their experience. Costs go down because the right decisions are made on the spot. Revenue soars as loyal customers increase their business and new customers actively seek you out.

When you apply our Eight Vital Insights you unleash the power of the individual, renew commitment and enthusiasm, and capture the hearts, minds, and courage of your people. Your bottom line dramatically improves and you are Turned On!

Epilogue: Wall Street was wrong. As we went to press Marriott had rebounded strongly—its stock price increasing 767 percent since that November 1990 meeting . . .

Turned On

ENTHUSIASTIC
CUSTOMERS

INSPIRED
PEOPLE

FINANCIAL
PERFORMANCE

8. Lead with Care

7. Unleash the Power of People

6. Measure Well, Act Fast

5. Make Technology Your Servant

4. Simplify, Simplify, Simplify

3. Have the Courage to Set Bold Goals

2. Make Every Customer Feel Special

1. Build a Strong Foundation

Insight 1

Build a Strong Foundation

"What's wrong with hospitals is that the people in charge don't think about what it's like to be a patient in that bed," says Mark Scott, CEO of Mid-Columbia Medical Center. "Here it's different. But don't ask me—talk to the people. You'll hear it from the heart. This place is on fire!"

Sue Kelly, a nurse at the hospital for twenty-two years, was an integral part of Mid-Columbia's radical transformation to patient-centered health care:

Nurses are nurturing, giving, and healing people, but the system turned us into task-oriented technicians. Schedules and tasks became more important than the patient. Since the change to patient-centered care I've experienced incredible personal growth. I'm alive again. I'm energized and passionate about what I do. Now I make a

1

tremendous difference in the lives of people every day, and they in turn make a difference for me. I go home, I'm charged. I come to work, I'm excited about being here.

I have a thank-you letter that I've saved for a long time. It's written by the daughter of a patient who spent her last days here. She writes, "Thank you for providing my sister and me with the experience of a lifetime. It has been the highlight of my life. I will never forget what you have done for us all."

This is why I went into health care.

JUST WHAT THE PATIENT ORDERED

Mid-Columbia Medical Center, a small rural hospital in The Dalles, Oregon, delivers health care as everyone would like it to be. Mid-Columbia's approach to patient-centered care was developed in conjunction with the Planetree Organization, a nonprofit consumer movement in San Francisco, as one of the five original Planetree demonstration sites in the nation.

Planetree rekindles the art and science of medicine. In the fifth century B.C. legendary healing centers like those at Kos and Epidaurus were temples filled with beautiful statues, fountains, and artistic treasures. Patients were surrounded by art, music, and poetry. Hippocrates' first schools of medicine were temples such as these. For centuries healing meant treating the *whole* patient—his or her physical, emotional, mental, and spiritual needs. In this century we've focused on revolutionizing the science of medicine, not the art of healing. By combining the advanced medical technology of today with the healing environments and relationships of the past, Mid-Columbia transforms the patient experience.

The journey meant rethinking, redesigning, and rebuilding every aspect of the care it provides. The first thing any organization must do is build a strong foundation consisting of five fundamental practices.

- **Pinpoint the essence of your business.** When you enter Mid-Columbia's atrium, with its waterfall and grand piano, you know right away you're not in a typical hospital. And when you see the patient rooms with their huge picture windows and meet people like Nurse Kelly, you understand that Mid-Columbia is in the business of wellness, not illness. The hospital built a complete healing environment for the community. Its focus on wellness is embodied by the acronym *HEALTH: H*umanistic care, *E*mpowerment, *A*ccess to information, *L*iberty to choose, *T*rust, and *H*eal.

- **Know your customers and their needs.** The Mid-Columbia staff knows its patients personally and devotes resources to meeting their special needs. Patients and their families, for example, have a profound desire to understand their condition and be

3

actively involved in their treatment. Rather than keep medical charts off-limits, doctors at Mid-Columbia invite patients to read their own charts, encouraging questions about medications and alternative treatments. Patients can visit the Health Resource Center for even more information—in English, not hospitalese.

- **Organize your business around your customers.** Mid-Columbia reorganizes the way work gets done to promote wellness and better meet the needs of its patients. Most hospitals wake patients in the middle of the night for blood tests because doctors need the lab results before they make their rounds. But patients sleep soundly at Mid-Columbia and doctors get lab results on time thanks to innovative staffing that puts more people in the laboratory at peak hours.
- **Have a clear and compelling mission.** Mid-Columbia's mission, "Personalize, humanize, and demystify health care," gives Nurse Kelly the direction and freedom to do whatever it takes to care for her patients.
- **Be brilliant on the basics.** Waterfalls and grand pianos don't mean much if patients aren't being healed. The basics are a careful blending of the latest expert medical care with a concern for the patient and family experience.

A strong foundation supports the framework of your business—when the fundamentals aren't right, nothing else will be. But changes in customer needs, technology, and the business environment mandate constant attention to your foundation.

Practice 1 PINPOINT THE ESSENCE OF YOUR BUSINESS

Practice 2 HAVE AN AFFAIR WITH YOUR CUSTOMER

Practice 3 SHAPE UP—PHYSICALLY AND MENTALLY

Practice 4 YOUR MISSION, SHOULD YOU CHOOSE TO ACCEPT IT . . .

Practice 5 BE BRILLIANT ON THE BASICS

Insight 1: Build a Strong Foundation

Practice 1

Pinpoint the Essence of Your Business

If Sports Illustrated *magazine understood it was in the sports information business, not the publishing business, we would have the Sports Illustrated Channel, not ESPN.*

—RON POBUDA,
National Audiovisual Association

Many companies define the scope of their business far too narrowly, thereby limiting their possibilities. When you pinpoint the essence of your business, you open up a new world of clarity and opportunity to explore. Think big, but start small.

A LASER FOCUS

Rural/Metro Corporation is a rapidly growing public company that provides 911, general ambulance, fire protection, and other health and safety services in fifteen states. In its hometown of Scottsdale, Arizona, the fire-loss rate (structural and property loss due to fire) is 50 percent lower than the national average. *Rural/Metro provides such service at a cost of up to 50 percent less than its public sector counterparts.*

In 1948 Lou Witzeman was unable to get fire service in the unincorporated area outside of Phoenix. Undaunted, he decided to start his own private fire service. Going door-to-door selling subscriptions and talking to neighbors, Lou realized that his community needed a service that could respond effectively to any emergency, not just fires. With this laser focus on the essence of his business, Lou reinvented the emergency services industry.

Rural/Metro operates with excellence in ways unthinkable to traditional fire departments. "We don't try to define for people what an emergency is," says John Karolzak, fire chief of Pima County, Arizona. "Is an emergency a house fire, or having a heart attack? Of course it is. But isn't it also an emergency when you find a snake in your bedroom? Or when you're locked out of your car? Absolutely." Rural/Metro removes desert reptiles, provides lock-out service, vacuums the water when pipes break in your home, offers blood pressure checks at the station, gives home fire safety inspections, and more.

Oh yeah, and it fights fires, too. But only when it has to.

Rural/Metro focuses on prevention to save lives and money, viewing every fire as a prevention failure. Christmas trees, for example, are a notorious fire hazard. Rural/Metro attacks the problem in a creative and effective way. "Right before Christmas we build a room and put in furniture, wall hangings, stockings, and gifts under a tree," John explains. "Then we light it on fire for the five o'clock news. People get the idea. Basically what you're doing is taking a dead bush, wrapping it in electrical equipment, putting kindling underneath it, and sticking it in your living room. You need to pay attention to these things."

> *Life and business are in the spirit and understanding. How they are done may vary.*
>
> —BILL COONEY, President, Property and Casualty Insurance, USAA

When fires do occur, the critical factor is not how many people are sitting in the station but how many are at the scene fighting the fire. Rural/Metro uses innovative staffing to get firefighters to the scene on time at significantly less cost. In addition to a smaller number of full-time firefighters at the station, Rural/Metro has a network of fully trained part-timers and reserves equipped with pagers. When a fire occurs in a metro area, the first firefighters are on their way to the scene less than ninety seconds after receiving a call. Within five minutes of their arrival, fifteen to twenty reserve firefighters will have joined them. Contrast this with almost every municipal fire station in the United States, where up to twenty full-time firefighters sit around and wait for a fire. "They're paying lots of money for a standing army," says Jim Bolin, president of Rural/Metro. "Our operation is based on an elite, agile, guerrilla warfare approach."

Because it truly understands the essence of its business, Rural/Metro transcends the traditional role of the local fire department. The company redefines the very concept of emergency, prevents fires whenever it can, and staffs creatively to fight fires effectively and cut costs.

MAKING PEOPLE FEEL GOOD

Mary Kay Cosmetics also transcends traditional definitions. You might think that the multibillion-dollar global organization is in the business of selling makeup. But spend five minutes with anyone associated with Mary Kay and the essence of its business comes shining through. "Selling is the transference of feeling," says Kathy Helou, a national sales director. "We're in the business of making people feel good."

Mary Kay showers its customers and its community with positive energy. "A therapist asked me to do a class for some women who were psychiatric patients," remembers Joan Brunner, another national sales director:

She warned me, "You're not going to sell anything, but perhaps you can help me connect with these women. They're so withdrawn they won't comb their hair, get dressed, or even respond." I did the class, though, because what you give out to the lives of others comes back to you tenfold. Everyone talked to me except for one woman. I asked her name and she finally whispered, "Anita."

When the class was over, everyone except Anita thanked me. But a minute later she walked back into the room, reached out, and touched me on the arm. She said, "Thank you. I really like me." Well, the therapist almost fainted—she had never seen Anita reach out to another human being. And the next morning, all the ladies dragged out the makeup bags their families packed for them months ago when they were sent to the hospital and had a blast. As for Anita, she was out of there a few weeks later.

HITTING THE NAIL ON THE HEAD

Neighborhood hardware stores are losing the price war to the Home Depots of the world, but Cole Hardware in San Francisco is winning—and not on the price of nails and screws. The company defines the essence of its business to be the problem-solver of the community.

Cole Hardware's directory of customer services is exhaustive. It includes:

- Free delivery anywhere in the city, free chauffeur service for senior citizens, and free plant repotting.
- Free use of Polaroid cameras to document damage or better describe a problem and free helium balloons for kids.
- Twenty-four-hour emergency plumbing, fire damage, and board-up service.
- Fax and e-mail service.

- A listing of approved local contractors who can do any job, big or small.

The complete list of services takes up an entire page in the Cole Hardware monthly newsletter. The small print in the bottom right corner reads, "By the way, we sell hardware, too."

When people have no idea how to solve a problem, they call Cole Hardware. One neighbor wondered if he was allowed to paint over the graffiti on the U.S. mailbox in front of his house. The sleuths at Cole Hardware called the government and discovered that repainting mailboxes is not only perfectly fine, but encouraged. The government even provides the matching shade of paint. Cole Hardware scanned the color into its paint system as "mailbox blue," and anyone interested can come down and get the paint for free.

Cole Hardware also developed a community and school assistance program. Purchases by a participating organization's constituents are tracked, and 10 percent of the revenues are returned to the group each month. The store also hosts after-hours fund-raisers for its partner organizations, from which 20 percent of all sales are returned. Last year alone Cole Hardware gave $24,000 back to the community.

Rural/Metro, Mary Kay Cosmetics, and Cole Hardware pinpoint the essence of their businesses. They think big about the possibilities and take small steps to achieve them. Do you define your business too narrowly? What opportunities are you missing?

INSIGHT TO ACTION

Insight 1: Build a Strong Foundation

Pinpoint the Essence of Your Business

❑ What does your company sell or make? What service do you provide? (e.g., We sell software.)

❑ What is the overarching purpose of your business? (e.g., help people work better, faster, and easier.)

❑ What basic expectations do customers have for your product or service? (e.g., ease of use and defect free.)

❑ How can you add value to differentiate your business? (e.g., on-site service, twenty-four-hour hotline, increased productivity.)

• _____

Practice 2

Have an Affair with Your Customer

You want to be where everybody knows your name.

—Theme song from *Cheers*

Every time the regulars enter the bar on the TV show *Cheers*, they're greeted by a rousing chorus of "Norm!" or "Cliff!" and served their favorite brew without having to ask. The bar knows its patrons and their needs and gets lifelong loyalty in return. But ask companies, "Who are your top customers?" and more often than not the eyes glaze over.

Make it your business to know your customers personally. Go beyond names and phone numbers—learn who your best customers are, what's important to them, and how to meet their individual needs.

KNOWLEDGE IS POWER

Truly knowing your customers means answering the following five questions:

- **Who uses your product or service, who pays for it, and who influences the decision to buy?** These aren't always the same people—it's crucial to differentiate among them. Consider the time Roger went computer shopping with his twelve-year-old son, Blake. "First we went to a warehouse store that sold all the popular brands. The salesperson bombarded me with logical reasons for buying my son an IBM or IBM-compatible product. At the second stop, an Apple store, the salesperson immediately sat Blake down in front of a computer. 'Let me show you how easy this is to use. Look at this neat game! You can research dinosaurs for your school reports like this.' As we left the store, Blake elbowed me in the ribs. 'You know which one we're buying, right Dad?'"

  The Apple salesman recognized that although Roger would be paying for the computer, Blake would be using it—and had the most influence on the purchase decision.

- **Do you have more than one customer?** Hospitals, for example, must satisfy the specific needs of several customer groups at once. Doctors, patients, and families all have different requirements, and don't forget the insurance companies who pay the bills.

14

- **Do you have an ongoing dialogue with customers?** Understand and anticipate the changing needs of customers. Involve customers in the design of new products and services.

- **Who are your best customers?** If your company is typical, the top 20 percent of your customers produce 80 percent of your business. It pays to know who they are and what's most important to them, and to devote enough time, money, and attention to retain their loyalty.

- **While you're busy chasing new customers, are loyal customers forgotten?** "Special introductory offer—6.9 percent APR for the first six months and no annual fee!" Why penalize faithful customers by giving only newcomers the hot deal? Get new customers, but keep the loyal ones enthusiastic. According to Technical Assistance Research Programs (TARP), it costs 5.7 times more to get a new customer than to retain a devoted one.

ARE YOU HAVING AN AFFAIR?

USAA is a $38-billion insurance and financial services organization that provides coverage to 2.6 million military personnel and their families. You might think that such a large insurance company wouldn't know its customers as anything more than account numbers. However, USAA's desire to know its customers is, well, passionate. "Business affairs" means something different to Bill Cooney, president of USAA's Property and Casualty Insurance Group. "Good companies have relationships with their customers. Great ones have lifetime affairs. And if you're going to have an affair, you've got to know your partner really well and anticipate his or her needs. You can't keep asking the same stupid questions like, 'When's your birthday?' It ruins the relationship. You know, it's just basic, simple stuff!"

Is your company ready to make this kind of commitment? Consider how deeply USAA nurtures its customer relationships:

- **Unconditional loyalty.** Members returning from the Gulf War were surprised to receive a prorated refund check on their automobile premiums, along with a note: "We're sure you couldn't have been driving your car a lot while you were in the Persian Gulf, therefore we don't want to charge you for carrying insurance you didn't use." Do you think another insurance company has any chance of stealing away USAA's customers?

- **Perfect timing.** Our research assistant, Jenny Lasser, has automobile coverage under her mother's policy. She notified USAA of her address change after graduating from college. USAA immediately sent an MTV-style handbook. "Now that you're out in the real world, here's some information to help you think

16

through renter's insurance and financial planning." USAA anticipated Jenny's changing needs and offered services in her language. As William Butler Yeats wrote, "Think like a wise man, but communicate in the language of the people."

- **Incredible responsiveness.** At USAA, responding to letters and mailing surveys isn't good enough. The company has an ongoing dialogue with its customers. Its automated ECHO program (*E*very *C*ontact *H*as *O*pportunity) records every customer comment, written or phoned in, good or bad, and the people at USAA immediately do something about it! Customer feedback is captured in a centralized database, enabling USAA to modify products and services and anticipate members' needs.

"We've got a strategic advantage," says Tim Timmerman, executive director for member relations and feedback. "Our customers talk to us. It would scare us to death if one day the phone stopped ringing. We'll take all the negative comments. We'll take all the positive comments. But just keep talking to us, customers."

LEARNING HOW TO LISTEN

Intel, the number one semiconductor company in the world, viewed original equipment manufacturers (OEMs) as its primary customers—even as Pentium Processors danced their way down a computer conga line in the popular "Intel Inside" commercials. The company brilliantly targeted home buyers, but when the infamous floating-point problem was broadcast over the Internet, Intel wasn't prepared to address their concerns.

> I've never gotten a referral from an unhappy customer. Once we abuse our customers' sensitivity, once we've sold them something that was averse to their interest—we've blown this entire business.
>
> —CHARLES SCHWAB,
> Chairman and CEO,
> The Charles Schwab
> Corporation

"End users knew the Intel name and depended on us to do the right thing," explains Craig Barrett, COO of Intel. "They heard about the flaw and felt like there was a real problem, but we were saying there wasn't one. We were out there with a bunch of technical mumbo jumbo that people couldn't understand. The consumer was counting on us to say, 'Hey, I understand there's a problem. We'll replace it.' Once we stopped trying to convince ourselves that we were right, we finally said exactly that and everything died overnight."

Intel learned to listen to the needs of its new customer—the home-PC buyer. Craig says the company is stronger for the experience. "We really got an education about what our end users are like and what they hold to be important. We've learned a lot and grown a lot." As a result, Intel now has the capability to handle the needs of *all* its customers. The Pentium's reputation is no worse for the experience, either. In fact, Intel touts the chip with its new logo: "Intel Inside: Pentium Processor."

Picture going on a date with two different people. One runs to the door with flowers and candy. The other toots the horn and expects you to run out to the car. Who are you going to want to see again? Are you running to your customer's door or just tooting your company horn?

INSIGHT TO ACTION

Insight 1: Build a Strong Foundation

Have an Affair with Your Customer

❑ Generate a list of the top 20 percent of your customers.

❑ Survey their preferences. (Speak personally with as many as possible.)

❑ Take three specific actions to improve your relationships (free upgrades, customer hotline, letter from the CEO, etc.).

• _____

• _____

• _____

❑ Have each top manager adopt a key account and build a personal relationship with it.

Practice 3

Shape Up—Physically and Mentally

Who hasn't been frustrated by being handed off from one person to another for service that should be handled in one stop? Too often the process is designed for the convenience of the business, not the customer. No one goes to a store to return, buy, and gift wrap in three different departments—they just want to shop. Shape up physically and mentally.

- **Organize around the customer.** Arrange your people and their work flow from the customer's point of view. Rearrange work spaces and customer areas to eliminate barriers, snags, and disconnects between what the customer wants and what you deliver.
- **Spend money on the right stuff.** Don't spend a dollar unless it ultimately benefits your customers—and start with your best customers.

- **Prepare for change.** Shaping up includes mental preparation. "Your people must understand why you're making an organizational change," says Larry Murphy, vice president of Marriott. "When you design everything around customer needs and get your people involved right from the start, you get automatic buy-in along with results."

THINKING LIKE A CUSTOMER

Organizing around the customer requires a huge shift in thinking about how you deliver your services. In the hotel industry, easy check-in is one of the most important factors in a guest's decision to return. Research indicated that Marriott had the highest check-in satisfaction ratings in its segment. But the scores had plateaued at 87 percent. An improved check-in process would mean more guests coming back, so Marriott began talking to customers, staff, and even people outside its industry. The company discovered three major problems:

- Marriott defined check-in as what specifically took place at the front desk. Customers, however, said that check-in included every step from making a reservation to locking the door to their rooms.
- Customers hated being handed off from valet to doorman to front-desk clerk to bellman—tipping all the way and repeating information. Staff members were

frustrated as well—they wanted to spend quality time with their guests.

• Customers often arrived to find that their rooms weren't ready because Marriott didn't know what time to expect them. Additionally, housekeepers claimed that working alone to make up room after room made their jobs boring and slow.

"First 10," Marriott's redesigned check-in process, focuses on the critical first ten minutes the guest spends in the hotel. Having learned that customers consider making a reservation to be part of the check-in process, Marriott physically linked its reservation and check-in systems. Marriott now asks for room preference, estimated time of arrival, and credit card information only once, when a guest calls for a reservation.

The daily list of guest arrivals is now printed in order of arrival so the hotel knows which rooms to prepare first. Housekeepers pointed out that it's easier and faster to make a bed with two people rather than have one person running around a king-size bed. So Marriott is testing housekeeping teams. Housekeepers in teams miss work less often because they like the new way of working and don't want to let their teammate down—an unforeseen benefit.

First 10 combines the doorman, bell staff, and front desk positions into what Marriott calls a "guest service agent." Now one person stays with a guest right through the redesigned check-in process. He or she meets the guest at the hotel entrance, grabs the guest's prepared portfolio, and takes the guest directly to the type of room requested. The customer gets through the critical first ten minutes fast and hassle-free.

The bottom line is that First 10 enthuses guests. "We consider a 1 percent improvement in our guest satisfaction score statistically significant," explains Larry Murphy. "Using this process, we have individual hotels exceeding 15 percent improvement in check-in satisfaction scores, which is the most dramatic in the history of our company—for any

> *The quickest way to profits is to serve the customer in ways that the customer wants to be served.*
>
> —ALFRED SLOAN,
> Chairman,
> General
> Motors, 1927

category." Marriott spends its money on the right stuff and has broken the 87 percent barrier. Overall check-in satisfaction is currently 94 percent.

SMALL-TOWN SERVICE, BIG-TIME RESULTS

Sewell Lexus in Dallas is doing even better, with a phenomenal 97.6 percent customer satisfaction index—largely because of the high marks customers give for service and repairs. The company learned how to do a better job by taking a drive in the country.

Small-town dealerships always posted much higher customer satisfaction ratings for service and repairs than anyone else in the industry. Sewell Motor Company President

Carl Sewell and his team studied small-town dealerships carefully to learn how they did it. "At these smaller, rural dealerships," says Carl, "you drive into the middle of the service department where the service manager meets you, writes your repair order, and hands it to the technician that best knows how to do the job. The service manager has a clear view of the technician, your car, and the parts department. He is right in the middle of everything. Well, rural dealerships only had four or five technicians. We've got forty or fifty, and they were so spread out you couldn't see squat!"

So Sewell Motor Company designed its new Lexus building to put service advisors close to the action. "We put the customer service drive-up and the technicians in the same building," explains Carl. "We use glass walls and put the service advisors' offices right between the drive lane and the technicians. Now a service advisor can see your car, the technician, the parts department, and *you* when you drive in for service and when you pick up your car. He's now personally involved in everything—just like the service manager in the small-town dealership."

Take a look at your operation. What steps and people are getting in the way? Eliminate them.

INSIGHT TO ACTION

Insight 1: Build a Strong Foundation

Shape Up—Physically and Mentally

❑ Pull together people, customers, and suppliers. Ask, "What three parts of our service frustrate you?"

People	Customers	Suppliers
_____	_____	_____
_____	_____	_____
_____	_____	_____

❑ Eliminate them.

❑ This is not a one-time fix. Customer expectations constantly change. Repeat every six months.

Practice 4

Your Mission, Should You Choose to Accept It . . .

On a consulting assignment with a company in the highly competitive software industry, Sue conducted focus groups with employees to discover why the company's performance and morale were sagging. She asked what the company's mission was. "Oh, we're not allowed to know that," an employee replied. "We're told it's confidential . . . "

Shopkeepers of times past had mission statements. They were clear, simple, and, most important, known throughout the village. The butcher's was "All the meat that's fit to eat." The baker's sign read, "Fresh, hot bread every day." But as the village became a town, and the town became a city, clear mission statements disappeared into a growing bureaucracy. Suddenly, drafting a company mission statement was "mission impossible." Committees were formed; gurus were consulted. Your statement had to *make* a statement. It had to say who you were, what you stood for, what you did, where you wanted to go, and how you were going to get there. It had to mention customers, vendors, suppliers, employees, owners, shareholders, and the community. It had to be powerful, but not so strong that it might offend someone. It had to be complete, yet short enough to fit on a mug. So companies gained mission statements, but the heart and soul of the business got lost in the translation.

Leverage the power of a clear and simple mission. Your mission statement is an indispensable tool when it:

- **Represents the heart and soul of the business.**
- **Is crisp, clear, and memorable.**
- **Is implementable and lived daily.**

The real test of a successful mission lies not in its form but in its spirit—whether your people know it, feel it in their hearts, and can fulfill it.

MISSION ACCOMPLISHED

When corporate headquarters dispatched the new company mission statement, it landed at the San Antonio River

Center Marriott with a thud. The document—seven pages of great ideas and inspirational goals—was about six-and-a-half pages too long. "On the cover page were four or five bullet points about the vision for that year," remembers General Manager Arthur Coulombe. "Buried in one of those bullet points was the phrase, 'Every guest leaves satisfied.' You can be sure that a lot of hotels read that memo and that was about the end of

> *People will support that which they help to create.*
>
> —KATHY HELOU,
> National Sales Director,
> Mary Kay Cosmetics

it. Our hotel, however, took that one phrase as our credo. We'd been searching for something very crisp, short, and understandable to provide direction for everybody—from the general manager to the cooks in the kitchen. Clarifying our mission was the start of something big."

The San Antonio River Center Marriott uses the simple, empowering credo "every guest leaves satisfied" to align its people around the heart and soul of the business. Associates know the mission, and they're given the tools and the freedom to do whatever it takes to fulfill it.

"We all bring out smiles in our guests in our own special way," says Marvin Martinez, a bellman and front-desk agent. "Me, I'm a performer. Every day I'm on stage in front of my biggest fans, my guests. When I walk out onto the floor, I am 'on.' I am an aggressive hospitality animal—my guests always leave satisfied!"

Associates who encounter unhappy guests solve the problem on the spot without going up the chain of command. They have an arsenal of products and services at their disposal (including a free night's stay, a free dinner, or a gift certificate for a future weekend stay) to smooth over difficult situations. But this isn't a giant giveaway program. Associates track problems so each department can make sure they don't happen again.

Marriott research confirms that giving people personal ownership of every guest leaving satisfied pays off. When a problem is handled immediately, intent to return increases dramatically.

GUEST EXPERIENCE	INTENT TO RETURN
No problems encountered during stay	89 percent
Had problem—fixed during stay	94 percent
Had problem—not remedied	69 percent

Another bellman, comparing the River Center Marriott to the hotel where he used to work, proudly stated, "Here the managers let you do what you gotta do!" That's why the San Antonio River Center Marriott has one of the highest guest satisfaction ratings in the Marriott chain—and also brings in the highest percentage profit.

HUMANIZE, PERSONALIZE, AND DEMYSTIFY

Mid-Columbia Medical Center also harnesses the power of living a simple mission statement. "When CEOs from other hospitals come to benchmark," says Mark Scott, "I ask them about their own values and missions. I get the typical, 'We're going to be the biggest, the mostest, the toughest, and we're going to gobble everyone else up.' Frankly, the mission here at Mid-Columbia used to be pretty similar. Now our mission is very clear. 'Humanize, personalize, and demystify health care.' Plain and simple."

This mission allows the staff to care for patients as human beings and to live by human values. When a patient asked if he could go to the atrium to hear the piano, Nurse Sue Kelly could do what she knew was right. "I had to hook up all of his pumps down there—it probably took me fifteen minutes. Then I played for him. He cried and cried. He was a strong forty-five-year-old dad dying of cancer, and wouldn't let his feelings out for fear his family would see them. The music just helped him to tap into his feelings, and he let go. That's probably the best thing that happened to him that day—in fact, I'm sure of it. And nobody's going to say, 'What is she doing playing the piano? Aren't we paying her twenty-five dollars an hour to work?'" People drive past other hospitals to come to Mid-Columbia. Wouldn't you?

A mission is whatever it takes to unite people around a common understanding that guides their actions. A general statement like "We're going to be the biggest and the mostest" does not guide employees in their day-to-day actions. But when a patient asks Nurse Kelly to play the piano, she immediately looks to "humanize and personalize health care," and knows exactly what to do.

THE LITMUS TEST

Legend has it that when Les Wexner, chairman of The Limited, was designing the Victoria's Secret stores, he was stumped trying to explain what the new stores were all about. He wanted the layout of the store, the interior design, and the merchandise displays to reflect a certain look and feel. One day, in a large department store, he noticed that all the lingerie hung from cheap acrylic hangers on cold aluminum garment stands. He thought, "I wonder if Cybill Shepherd is comfortable buying her underwear like this?"

Les Wexner pulled his team together and instructed, "We're designing a store where Cybill Shepherd would love to shop for lingerie." That clear picture enabled The Limited to develop the entire Victoria's Secret concept— from store layout to decor to catalogs to displays. Whenever the design team had a question, its members asked themselves, "Would Cybill like this?" Who can play the role of Cybill Shepherd for your business?

A litmus test uses a single indicator to prompt a decision, and that's exactly what a mission statement must do.
Whenever your people question the right thing to do, they
can look to the mission: Did my guest leave satisfied? Am
I treating my patient like a human being? Would Cybill
like this? What matters is that everybody knows, feels, and
understands what they need to do to live the mission—
and that the corporate culture supports their actions. As
each person lives the mission, decisions become easier,
teams become more autonomous, and the internal muscle
of the organization grows.

INSIGHT TO ACTION

Insight 1: Build a Strong Foundation

Your Mission, Should You Choose to Accept It . . .

❑ Write your company mission statement in fifteen or fewer simple, compelling words.

❑ Make sure it captures the heart and soul of your business.

❑ Insist that it guide every activity.

Practice 5

Be Brilliant
on the Basics

*The most important thing is to serve the hot food
hot and the cold food cold.*

—J. W. Marriott,
Founder, Marriott Corporation

You may have sunk $2 million into the decor of your
restaurant, but if the hot food is cold when it gets to the
table, you just lost a customer. If you're looking for ways
to add value but don't deliver the basics, you're wasting
your time and money.

What are the basics? They are the fundamental things
that decide whether or not a customer will continue to do
business with you. Be brilliant on the basics and customers
will tolerate everything else. Screw up on the basics and
nothing else matters—customers will not come back.
Period.

WHAT MATTERS MOST?

With your people and customers, fill in the blank: "Nothing else matters if we don't do _____ well." Marriott identified its basics by analyzing the results of a comprehensive guest survey. Its customers' intent to return rests on five critical factors:

- Everything is clean and works.
- Check-in is hassle-free.
- Staff is friendly and hospitable.
- Problems are resolved quickly.
- Breakfast is served on time.

When Marriott fails to deliver any of the above, the customer heads for the door. No amount of mints on the pillow will bring back a guest whose bathroom was dirty or whose television didn't work.

Being consistently brilliant on the basics lets you distinguish yourself in the marketplace. Marriott, for example, is the top choice for meeting planners and has the industry's best frequent traveler program. But the company developed these defining aspects of its business only after mastering the fundamentals.

Customers can also count on Southwest Airlines to

> *Everyone is looking for magic. But magic comes in doing the basic things well.*
>
> —JACQUE SCOTT, Administrative Director of Nursing Services, Mid-Columbia Medical Center

deliver the basics. Employees are always on stage, telling jokes, teasing passengers, and bursting into song. But what if attendants popped out of overhead bins for a laugh but flights ran thirty minutes late and your baggage went to Poughkeepsie more often than not? Suddenly that joke isn't funny anymore. But Southwest Airlines consistently excels at the fundamentals. In fact the company has won the airline industry's Triple Crown award four years running: it is number one in on-time arrival, unloading baggage quickly with the fewest bags lost, and overall customer satisfaction.

GET PEOPLE UP TO SPEED

At first glance, Intel seems light-years away from anything remotely basic. Forward thinking, forward acting, and fast-forward technology seem more appropriate watchwords. In fact, Intel's success is firmly grounded in the basics. However, the company's phenomenal rate of growth—it has added over 5,000 new employees in the last three years alone—diluted its relentless focus on the fundamentals. New employees didn't experience the dedication to basics that made Intel the number one company in the semiconductor industry.

In 1995 "Excel at Intel Basics" became one of three annual corporate objectives. "There is a vital need to integrate a vast number of new employees into the Intel culture," explains Dave Crowley of Intel's corporate quality network.

"'Back to Basics' is a return to what made us great."

Keith Erickson of Intel strategic materials maintains that "Back to Basics" will always be a top priority. "Consistent performance drives our business, so the basics are taken very seriously—it's our way of paying attention to every detail. We analyze the business and identify a basic for everyone to focus on for the coming year, whether it's performance management, training, being the supplier of choice, or meeting production requirements. In fact, our COO Craig Barrett considers Intel Basics such a high priority that it's a major topic of discussion during every meeting and site visit."

A company moving at Intel's speed must always focus on the fundamentals. But just because it's basic doesn't mean it's easy. It takes dedication and effort to stay on top. You may think you've got the basics mastered, but your customers and competitors are busy upping the ante. Southwest Airlines, for example, has been brilliant at on-time arrival and baggage handling. But its consistent focus on low price and fun elevates what customers expect from the rest of the industry. Make sure you're the one pushing the edge of the envelope.

INSIGHT TO ACTION

Insight 1: Build a Strong Foundation

Be Brilliant on the Basics

❏ Identify with customers the five areas necessary to keep their business.

- _____
- _____
- _____
- _____
- _____

❏ Keep a monthly scorecard of how you're doing on them. Share results with everyone.

❏ Conduct a "basics checkup" quarterly.

ENTHUSIASTIC
CUSTOMERS

INSPIRED
PEOPLE

FINANCIAL
PERFORMANCE

8. Lead with Care

7. Unleash the Power of People

6. Measure Well, Act Fast

5. Make Technology Your Servant

4. Simplify, Simplify, Simplify

3. Have the Courage to Set Bold Goals

2. Make Every Customer Feel Special

1. Build a Strong Foundation

Insight 2

Make Every Customer Feel Special

Dear Mr. Marriott,

I'd like to tell you about my recent experience in your Anaheim Marriott Hotel. After checking in, I ordered room service. A young man named Charles came up with my order. As I signed the check, he asked, "Ma'am, do you have allergies or have you been crying?"

"I've been crying," I replied. "My sister has been terminally ill and my brother just called to tell me she died while I was on the flight here. I need to go home right away, but the first flight isn't until eight A.M. So you see, I don't want to be

in your hotel tonight, but I have no choice. There's really nothing you can do."

Charles paused. "Well, I want you to know that you have my sympathy. If there's anything you need tonight, please don't hesitate to call me. It would be my pleasure."

Somehow, knowing that Charles the room-service waiter cared made me feel a little bit better. About forty-five minutes later Charles knocked at my door. I assumed he had returned for my tray, but he was holding another tray with a pot of coffee and a piece of warm apple pie.

"Our chef makes the best apple pie in the entire company. We heated up a piece for you—it's on us," he said. Then he reached into his pocket and pulled out a sympathy card.

I opened the card to find seven signatures. Charles told me who each person was and what they did at the hotel. He explained that these were his friends, and they kind of ran the place at night.

"We got you this card to let you know you're not alone tonight—lots of us care."

Mr. Marriott, I'll never meet you. And I don't need to meet you because I met Charles. I know what you stand for. I know what your values are. I want to assure you that as long as I live, I will stay at your hotels and tell my friends to stay at your hotels. That night I realized that you care *more about me as a person than you do about the few dollars I spent at your hotel . . .*

A HUMAN TRANSACTION

When was the last time a business made you feel special? Charles the room-service waiter tapped into the positive emotions we all feel when someone takes a caring, personal interest. Customers are human beings with unique emotions, needs, and desires, but business today is complex and automated. Products and services are standardized and formalized. Procedures and regulations overshadow people and relationships. Why do we continue to make one size to fit all? Why don't we treat people as individual human beings?

Charles the room-service waiter wasn't responding to his guest in accordance with any checklist or procedure. He simply treated her like a human being, giving personal service based on his understanding of her needs. After generations of mass production and assembly-line service, customers are starved for personal attention. Find innovative ways to tailor your products and handcraft your service. Just as Charles's customer swore her undying loyalty, so too will your customers if you treat them like human beings with individual needs and the power to choose.

We can no longer make one product, offer one service, or develop one relationship to satisfy everyone. The following practices present choices, customization, and personal relationships as the new rules. In addition, Insights 4 and 5 will demonstrate how simplification and technology work hand in hand to make customers feel special.

Practice 6   **GIVE CUSTOMERS THE POWER OF CHOICE**

Practice 7   **ONE SIZE DOESN'T FIT ALL**

Practice 8   **BE OBSESSED WITH PERSONAL RELATIONSHIPS**

Practice 6

Give Customers
the Power of Choice

Do you dread going to the DMV? After putting it off for weeks, you step in the front door and immediately find yourself in your first line—the one for the information desk. Each person in front of you has a different problem.

"Hi, I have to renew my registration."

"Line E."

"I got this notice in the mail, it says . . . "

"Line E."

"Hello, I . . . "

"Line E."

You are dispatched to Line E as well. It's kind of like being at Disneyland, except there's no ride.

One choice is no choice at all and only makes us feel frustrated and powerless. People have a fundamental need to choose for themselves—give your customers the power of choice.

LET YOUR CHOICE BE HEARD

When was the last time you had freedom of choice in, of all places, a hospital? Patients at Mid-Columbia Medical Center make choices every day. The hospital offers a menu of options and encourages substitutions. It's all part of the master plan to return power and dignity to the patient.

"I've been a nurse for twenty-three years," says Jacque Scott, administrative director of nursing services, "and patient gowns have always been one of the biggest issues. The patient gown is see-through, doesn't cover people of different sizes, and you never know how to put the thing on. It immediately says that not only are you sick but you're vulnerable. It's very difficult to feel safe when you're vulnerable. So the

> There are two thresholds of service. There is the minimum threshold: if you don't do this, then a customer can't and won't do business with you. Period. Then there's the "WOW" threshold and above that, the customer is blown away, amazed. Unbelievably fantastic. We try to pick those spots where we can differentiate ourselves—places that are important to the customer, where we can "WOW" them.
>
> —DAVID POTTRUCK,
> President and COO,
> The Charles Schwab
> Corporation

46

first thing we did is find a gown that actually covers people, that you can't see through, and that is still functional to do exams. People get to choose from coral, blue, green, hot pink, purple, and other really bright colors. We've tried to create a safe and healing environment by providing people with options."

At Mid-Columbia, selecting a gown is one of many choices that humanize the patient experience and get patients home faster.

- Patients choose a family member, friend, or even a volunteer to become their "care partner"—someone who learns about their condition and helps care for them in the hospital and later at home.
- Friends and family can stop by whenever they like, because visiting hours are twenty-four hours a day.
- Friends and family can cook for patients in the kitchens on every floor, provided patients are not on restricted diets.
- When patients do choose hospital food, they get to eat when they're hungry, not when it's convenient for the staff.
- Surgery patients can bring a tape of their favorite music to listen to on a Walkman as they go under anesthesia and as they wake up.
- There's a VCR in every room, and patients enjoy the use of a large video library.
- Patients can relax with massages, facials, or meditation.
- An art cart travels from room to room delivering a wide selection of activities.

- Patients can decorate their rooms the way they want by selecting artwork from a photo album.
- A portable fish tank can be wheeled in to any room.

Mid-Columbia even lets patients read their own medical charts. Unthinkable at most hospitals, access to charts has been nothing but positive. Mark Scott notices an increasing dialogue about healing and wellness, not to mention improved penmanship from doctors. "I remember that one patient was reading through his chart and saw what looked like 'S.O.B.' written in there somewhere. The patient burst out, 'What is this "S.O.B." all about? I haven't done anything!' The doctor started laughing. 'S.O.B. means "Shortness of Breath." We noticed it was hard for you to breathe when you came in yesterday.' They both had a good chuckle about the misunderstanding. But it was an important moment because it opened up a dialogue and a trust was formed."

Communication and trust come free when you provide customers with choices. And Mid-Columbia doesn't spend more money to provide choices, it just spends money more *wisely*, putting resources into products and services that directly affect the patient.

What is the impact of providing choices at Mid-Columbia?

- Patient satisfaction exceeds that of all area hospitals.
- Patients come from all over the country to receive care.

- The hospital attracts and keeps the best nurses— turnover is an extraordinarily low 3 percent.
- CEOs from other hospitals flock to Mid-Columbia to benchmark, and leave saying, "When I get sick, I'm coming here."

INSIGHT TO ACTION

Insight 2: Make Every Customer Feel Special

Give Customers the Power of Choice

❑ With staff, customers, and suppliers build a wish list of choices for each product and service.

❑ Track customer requests—they will lead to new products, services, and businesses.

❑ Recognize people who continually take initiative to provide choices.

❑ Check out choices and options offered by others. Improve on them.

Practice 7

One Size Doesn't Fit All

For decades companies sought the Holy Grail of economy of scale, attempting to crank out one product to please everyone. But we're all fed up with mass-market goods and faceless service. Tailor your products and handcraft your service to create outrageous value in the eyes of your customers—they'll gladly pay for it.

- **Increase share of customer, as well as share of market.** The most fertile ground to grow your business lies with existing customers. Work with each one to understand their current and future needs. Partner with customers to create unique, value-added solutions. Sell as many products as possible to each of them.

- **Treat every customer as the only customer.** Market segments don't buy anything—individuals do. Make every individual a distinct customer group, and start with your best customers. If you can't go all the way, make segments as small as possible.

51

CUT FROM A DIFFERENT CLOTH

After years of successfully mass producing its popular brands of clothing, Levi Strauss & Co. is turning back into the tailor next door. In 1849 Levi Strauss made custom blue jeans for prospectors during the gold rush. Today, in select locations around the world, the company he founded is making individually fitted women's jeans. As Bob Rockey, president of Levi Strauss & Co. North America, observed, "The more things change, the more they stay the same."

For about twenty dollars more than an off-the-shelf pair, customers can help design their own pair of Levi's. A salesperson enters individual measurements into a computer linked to a fabric-cutting machine at the sewing factory. Within two weeks customers get the brand name they know and love in a pair of jeans fitted to their liking.

By partnering with customers Levi Strauss & Co. creates value-added solutions and increases its share of customer. The only thing the company is shrinking is the two-week wait.

Levi Strauss & Co. customizes its service for retail stores as well. The company's current $850 million reengineering project features programs to assist retail owners in growing sales and increasing profits. Responding to retailer requests, the company provides customized point-of-sale materials and display fixtures. Most important, Levi Strauss & Co. ships merchandise floor-ready—folded and tagged exactly as individual stores want it. This seamless combination of old-fashioned service and mass-production capability strategically strengthens Levi Strauss & Co.'s position as the top apparel manufacturer in the world.

MAKE A STATEMENT

The Charles Schwab Corporation of San Francisco is the nation's biggest discount broker. In the last four years revenue more than doubled to $1.4 billion, net income more than tripled to $173 billion, and stock prices shot up from less than 6 to the mid-20s. Like Levi Strauss & Co., Charles Schwab provides cost-effective personal service on a mass scale. "As the company got

> *I can't give you a sure-fire formula for success, but I can give you a sure-fire formula for failure: try to please everybody all the time.*
>
> —HERBERT BAYARD SWOPE

bigger and more successful," says Tom Seip, executive vice president of retail, "it became real clear that with a 'one size fits all' approach, we would not continue to flourish. We split up into segments called 'customer enterprises' to best take care of each type of customer."

But even clients grouped into the same customer enterprise have vastly different needs. Consider investment managers—financial advisors using Schwab to handle their clients' financial transactions. John Coghlan, executive vice president of Schwab Institutional, says the company asked these advisors about their specific requirements and quickly discovered how diverse they were. "Thats why we let financial advisors design their own

53

statements. For some, being affiliated with Charles Schwab is a big plus, so they can have the regular Schwab statement with their name on it somewhere. Other advisors can elect to have their own logo front and center and a less prominent Schwab logo—I mean, we're not going to put it on the back, but we'll at least put it at the bottom in really small type."

From designing a statement to back-office and marketing-support needs, Schwab's enterprise for investment managers is a flexible, manageable system that offers tailored solutions. "We've created a sort of cafeteria line," explains John. "Financial advisors can come in and pick the various elements that make sense to them, and then pay only for that. But we've also packaged certain things together that should appeal to specific types of advisors—you know, a couple of blue plate specials. Tuesday is turkey, and so on. If you don't want the special, that's okay. You can still choose whatever is best for you."

Charles Schwab does more than group customers into segments. It creates a system flexible enough to meet the individual needs of every investment manager—a segment of one.

JUST LIKE AUNT BARBARA DOES IT

Our research assistant's Aunt Barbara is famous for her stellar hospitality. She always serves your favorite dishes, and never the same thing twice. That's because, in the dusty old shoe boxes in her pantry, she has an index card listing the likes and dislikes of every single person who's come to dinner or tea since 1968!

The Ritz-Carlton Hotel Company uses exactly the same method to dazzle its guests. Employees note each guest's favorite foods, snacks, beverages, kind of pillow, and room temperature—*anything* that would make their stay better. But Ritz-Carlton doesn't have shoe boxes. Instead, it puts the information into a computerized guest preferences tracking system shared among properties worldwide.

The Ritz-Carlton is even more proactive with top customers. It calls secretaries ahead of time to get a list of a VIP's special favorites. When the VIP arrives, every employee in the hotel has a copy of that list. "Our goal is to achieve 100 percent customer loyalty," says president and COO Horst Schulze. "The only way to get there is to provide personal, one-to-one service. To do that we must anticipate the needs of our guests."

The commitment to tailored products and handcrafted service at The Ritz-Carlton, Charles Schwab, and Levi Strauss & Co. sounds extravagant. But Aunt Barbara has heard it all before. "People ask me, 'How can you keep track of all that? It must take so much time!' But really it just takes a few seconds. I'm going to cook in any case, so I may as well make them what they want."

Words to live by. *You're going to serve those customers in any case, so you may as well give them what they want.*

INSIGHT TO ACTION

Insight 2: Make Every Customer Feel Special

One Size Doesn't Fit All

❑ Identify three ways to provide personal services for customers.

- _____
- _____
- _____

❑ Focus resources and systems cost-effectively to deliver what customers want (i.e., bill customers the way they want—you will get your money faster).

❑ Define and test three new ways to build share of customer.

- _____
- _____
- _____

Practice 8

Be Obsessed with Personal Relationships

Don't open a shop unless you know how to smile.

—Jewish proverb

Charles the room-service waiter epitomizes the awesome power of human interaction. The personal relationship, not the warm apple pie, won the undying loyalty of his customer. Customers remember a personal relationship, and that keeps them coming back. What is your most memorable experience as a customer? Did it involve a product or was it someone who did something very special for you?

Quality products and service yield *satisfied* customers. A satisfied customer will only stay with you until someone else offers a slightly lower price, a little more convenience, or improves the product a bit. Quality relationships create *enthusiastic* customers, directly strengthening your current and future bottom line. When you have enthusiastic customers, you create a bond that's virtually impossible for competitors to break.

- **Enthusiastic customers are forgiving when you make a mistake.**
- **You never have to "sell" them—they seek you out.**
- **They provide an endless source of great new ideas.**
- **Your best advertising is their word of mouth.**

A LIFETIME OF DEVOTION

The Mary Kay experience is one that people never forget. Millions of people worldwide use Mary Kay products, but the company's most immediate customers are its 450,000 independent sales associates. Mary Kay Cosmetics treats every associate like family. "The company is my life, and these people are my daughters," explains Mary Kay Ash, founder and chairman. "I always say that and I mean it. They call me all the time on weekends to ask for my help and advice. It's as if my own daughter was calling. I do my best to try to give them the same advice I would give to any member of my family. They are my family."

Mary Kay builds her "family" relationships with sincerity and integrity.

A SALES ASSOCIATE IS:

- the most important person in our business. She is our only customer.
- dependent on us, and we are dependent on her.
- not an interruption of our work. She is the purpose of it.
- not a cold statistic. She is a flesh-and-blood human being with feelings and emotions like our own.
- deserving of the most courteous and attentive treatment we can give.
- the lifeblood of this business.

—Mary Kay Cosmetics philosophy

Change the words "sales associate" into "customer" and then "our people." Adopt the credo for your company. What would you do differently?

Mary Kay Cosmetics makes everyone feel special. "Every single person you meet has a sign around his or her neck that says, 'Make Me Feel Important,'" insists Mary Kay Ash. "If you can do that, it's amazing the results you get."

This corporate philosophy

> [Regarding Harley Davidson] When you can get customers to tattoo your logo on their arms and chests—that's customer enthusiasm.
>
> —JACK SMITH, Chairman, General Motors

nurtures a deep-seated commitment. Rose Grubich of Finleyville, Pennsylvania, joined Mary Kay at the age of sixty-five and quickly became one of the top salespeople in town. She had just won her first Red Jacket, a Mary Kay honor signifying advancement in her career, when she learned of her terminal cancer.

That didn't stop Rose. She started selling cosmetics with renewed vigor. Even on her hospital deathbed, she sold night creme and facial cleanser to her nurses. When she passed away, she was buried in her Red Jacket as requested. Four pink Mary Kay Cadillacs and five red Mary Kay Pontiac Grand-Ams accompanied Rose to her final resting place. One mourner remarked, "It was the most amazing sight Finleyville has ever seen."

Imagine a customer of yours making a special request to be buried in your company's golf shirt . . .

People who use Mary Kay products become customers for life. "The product is great and really sells itself," said one customer. "But Tina, my consultant, is so much fun to be with. I really enjoy the times we get together." You must offer a quality product—that's a given. Offering human relationships differentiates you in your customer's heart and in the marketplace.

HUGS VERSUS DRUGS

An understanding of human relationships forever altered the lives of the residents of Coliseum Gardens in Oakland,

California. In 1991 when the murder rate in Oakland was the fourth highest in the nation, that of the Coliseum Gardens housing project was a frightening eleven times higher. Drug dealers, most of whom didn't even live there, had taken over the community. Gangsters drove through the complex at top speed, firing their guns out the windows as residents dropped to the floor and prayed. Cab drivers and pizza deliverymen refused to enter. The fire department demanded a police escort. After dark even the police wouldn't set foot in the housing project.

Residents lived in daily fear of the drug dealers, called "D-Boys." One resident left for the weekend and came back to find the D-Boys doing drugs and drinking beer in his living room.

"What are you doing here?" he stammered. "This is my house."

"Well, you better find yourself a new house," a dealer replied.

So he did. Every single resident in the community shared this feeling of helplessness.

> *Personal relationships and the ability to trust and understand each other is the bottom line of business. That's where all the leverage is.*
>
> —Chip Chipman,
> Vantage Consulting

All that changed when a group of trainers from the Health Realization Institute introduced the power of thought. Beverley Wilson, part of the three-member team, went to Coliseum Gardens to strengthen relationships and revive the spirit of hope. "If the residents could only reclaim the power within themselves, then rebuild the trust that had disintegrated over years of fear and neglect, they would be a force to reckon with."

61

Residents learned to recognize that the anxiety and helplessness that held them back were only *thoughts*, not *reality*. When people finally cast off their negative thoughts, they discovered common sense and optimism hidden underneath. Individuals grew strong, and their relationships and community quickly followed.

The health of the community, forged one relationship at a time, gradually displaced the drug dealers. Today the homicide rate is down 100 percent and violent crime is down nearly 50 percent. Drug possession is down 20 percent. Gang warfare and ethnic clashes have disappeared.

The statistics are impressive. The stories of how individual lives have changed are even more so. "We used to hold our resident meetings outside so that skeptics could see that we weren't doing anything top secret," recalls Beverley:

Every day Belle, who called herself the "Coliseum Gardens Alcoholic," would walk by our meeting. She'd say, "I'm going to get some beer or wine. Anyone got a dollar?" We'd always say, "No, but we do have a hug for you." And we'd all hug her. Pretty soon Belle asked us for hugs instead of a dollar! She'd say, "You didn't give me a hug today! What's wrong with you?" We never talked to her about her alcoholism because she didn't want to.

One day a lady was handing out flower seeds to anyone who wanted to start a garden. Well, Miss Belle said, "I'm going to go home and plant me a garden!" So she got out there and turned up the ground and started planting her flower garden. Now remember—this is the Coliseum Gardens Alcoholic! It was a sight to see, this woman out there planting, not drinking, cussing, or asking for money. One day she just said, "You know, I ain't had a drink in weeks. I just ain't thought about it, and I don't want it, and I don't need it. I feel good." And today flower gardens, inspired by Belle, go all the way around Coliseum Gardens.

IF YOU CAN MAKE IT THERE, YOU CAN MAKE IT ANYWHERE

Warm and fuzzy doesn't work in the business world, right? Joyce Davis, executive director of the Mount Hope Housing Project in the Bronx, would disagree. She too has seen the power of relationships at work.

Mount Hope was once a thriving community, one of peace and hope. A community that you would want to raise your children in. "All of a sudden, it just wasn't like that anymore," remembers Joyce. "We woke up one day to a war zone—abandoned buildings, crime, and drugs everywhere."

With a commitment to revitalize every facet of their community, Joyce Davis and a group of residents founded the Mount Hope Housing Project. They attracted banks and small businesses and refurbished a number of buildings. Most important, Mount Hope rebuilt relationships.

"People never related well to property managers," Joyce points out. "But now our property managers go into the community to talk with residents and build relationships. One of my managers, Miriam, has really connected. Residents don't see a 'property manager' anymore, they see Miriam. I have people walking into my office saying, 'I haven't paid my rent in six months, but I want to start now,' and it's because they don't want to get Miriam in trouble. It all translates into better business. We are 100 percent occupied—with a waiting list. Where we used to have 50 percent collections, we have almost 95 percent. Our expenses have gone down because we don't have to repaint graffiti-covered hallways and rebuild demolished buildings. People want to help themselves, and it means much less work for my maintenance and security folks. As manager of this housing project, I watch my bottom line. And I know that it has improved tremendously as the relationships improved."

If you think that personal relationships and understanding are only for inner-city communities, think again. That's what business is all about—a series of relationships among customers, suppliers, management, and employees. "The strength of those ties are a better predictor of what's going to come out the other end than a company's techniques, systems, and models," says Chip Chipman of Vantage Consulting, which applies Health Realization principles to business. What relationships could use some beefing up in your organization?

For Mount Hope, Coliseum Gardens, and Mary Kay Cosmetics, personal relationships are the building blocks of long-term vitality. An organization that develops strong and positive relationships unleashes a mighty force. As Joyce Davis says, "It's not just a good way to run a business, it's the only way to run a business."

INSIGHT TO ACTION

Insight 2: Make Every Customer Feel Special

Be Obsessed with Personal Relationships

❑ Adopt the Mary Kay philosophy to treat everyone like family. What two things will you do differently?

- _____

- _____

❑ List three associates, customers, and suppliers with whom to build and nurture a personal relationship:

Associates	Customers	Suppliers
_____	_____	_____
_____	_____	_____
_____	_____	_____

❑ Insist that your team do the same.

ENTHUSIASTIC
CUSTOMERS

INSPIRED
PEOPLE

FINANCIAL
PERFORMANCE

8. Lead with Care

7. Unleash the Power of People

6. Measure Well, Act Fast

5. Make Technology Your Servant

4. Simplify, Simplify, Simplify

3. Have the Courage to Set Bold Goals

2. Make Every Customer Feel Special

1. Build a Strong Foundation

Insight 3

Have the Courage to Set Bold Goals

Jim Whittaker is chairman of Greenway, a direct marketer of environmental products, former president and CEO of REI, a sports equipment cooperative, and the first American to reach the summit of Mt. Everest. To celebrate Earth Day 1990 Jim organized a Peace Climb to the top of Mt. Everest to demonstrate what can be achieved through friendship and cooperation. At the time, only the United States, China, and the Soviet Union had the nuclear capability to destroy the earth. Jim's goal was to see climbers from each of these rival nations embracing at the highest point in the world.

Assembling the team proved more difficult than imagined. Each country hesitated to send representatives, fearing its climbers wouldn't succeed. "We'll drag your people to the top if we have to," Jim promised. Finally, a small group of veteran climbers came forward, eager for the challenge. None had scaled Everest before.

Trust, unity, and attention to detail were paramount, but the team was far from united. No one spoke the same language—the group relied on interpreters. Climbers only trusted the equipment and know-how of their own nation. Which nation would provide the team doctor? The Americans declared, "I don't want to be 20,000 feet high, have something go wrong, and the only medical treatment available is acupuncture." The Chinese retorted, "We don't want some narrow-minded Western doctor." In the end, one doctor from each nation made the climb.

The climbers began to ascend the mountain, becoming a tight-knit team as the climb progressed. Each day they moved higher, until the atmosphere became dangerously thin—the death zone. One thought weighed heavily on everyone's mind: of the 200 people who'd reached the summit, more than 100 died there. But Jim pushed his group on. "When you play for more than you can afford to lose, you learn the game."

The final ascent was the most treacherous. A cornice caps the summit, and people have fallen through the lip of snow to their deaths. The danger is not knowing when to stop. But the group safely relayed twenty men and women to the top of Mt. Everest—a new record for a single team. The Peace Climb had reached the summit at last.

Jim Whittaker and his team accomplished the boldest of goals, the kind that stirs our blood and calls us to action. Jim's story evokes a time when the pioneering spirit was alive and the possibilities endless.

"Challenge is the core and mainspring of all human activity," says Jim. "If there is an ocean, we will cross it. If there is a wrong, we will right it. If there is a disease, we will cure it. If there is a mountain, we will climb it. If there is a company, you can make it the best. People ask me all the time why I run a business. It's for the same reason I climb a mountain—the challenge."

The pioneering spirit is often missing in business today. In its place broods the march of incre-mentality. There is safety in gradual change, but what dreams are you stifling? What triumphs are you limiting?

CAPTURE HEARTS AND MINDS

A bold goal must capture the hearts and minds of the people who do the real work, making them feel part of something bigger than themselves. Soon after John F. Kennedy announced that the United States would put a man on the moon, a janitor at NASA was asked to describe his job. "I am helping to put a man on the moon," he replied. In fact, all Americans believed they were putting a man on the moon. We didn't know how, but we'd find a way.

"It's not what's in front of you that blocks your way,"

says Jim Whittaker, "it's what's inside that holds you back." Which mountain does your organization need to climb?

Practice 9   **KEEP YOUR FEET ON THE GROUND AND YOUR HEAD IN THE STARS**

Practice 10   **COLOR OUTSIDE THE LINES**

Practice 11   **NO COMPANY IS AN ISLAND**

Practice 9

Keep Your Feet on the Ground and Your Head in the Stars

It takes all the running you can do to keep in the same place. If you want to go somewhere else, you must run at least twice as fast as that.

—LEWIS CARROLL,
Through the Looking Glass

Picture a giant walking through the countryside. His footsteps are firm, but his head is in the stars. He has a clear view of the landscape for miles around. The giant sees exactly where he wants to go, and moves closer with every step.

Companies with their feet on the ground and their heads in the stars become giants themselves. They have a panoramic planning process, and take firm and immediate steps to achieve their goals. Become a giant in your field.

- **Be bold when things are good.** Pursue your goals from a position of strength, not desperation. Desperate moves usually fail.
- **Break down your goal.** Identify the components of your goal with people, customers, and suppliers to achieve it step by step. Create teams responsible for each piece. Small wins are opportunities for learning, celebration, and inspiration.
- **Change your tire while going sixty miles per hour.** Make sure your company continues full speed ahead while you pursue your bold goal.

$850 MILLION IN CHANGE

Levi Strauss & Co. is the number one or number two brand leader in every market it operates in around the world. The company has set sales records for the last ten years and posted record earnings nine of those ten years. Yet Levi Strauss & Co. is undertaking an $850 million reengineering project. "We're extremely successful by every financial measure," says Tom Kasten, vice president of reengineering and customer service implementation. "So why go through a reengineering process?"

Three years ago Levi Strauss & Co. took a hard look at the service it provided to retail customers. The company sent teams to each of its major retail customers to talk with store executives, managers, salespeople, and warehouse staff. "We scored very high on the quality, uniqueness, and coolness of our products, and our marketing was fabulous," says Tom. "But our service left a lot to be desired. We had trouble getting our 'cool' products on the shelves for stores to sell. One retailer said, 'If you weren't Levi's, you'd be gone.'"

Levi Strauss & Co. faced the reality. "We thought, 'If we don't fix this, it could be our Achilles heel,'" says Tom. "Unlike General Motors or IBM, we could solve our problem when we were strong creatively and financially—what better time to fix it?" The company set a bold goal: to be the superior service provider in the world—not just in the apparel industry, but in all industries. "We want any company in the world to say, 'If you want to provide great customer service, you need to approach it like Levi Strauss & Co. does," explains Tom.

What would it take to be superior? Talking to retail customers made one thing totally clear—the

> *A great archer is only as good as his ability to identify his target. It doesn't do you any good as an organization to have a lot of great archers around if they don't know what the heck they are shooting at.*
>
> —RANDY CARTER, Director, MCMC University, Mid-Columbia Medical Center

73

supply chain had to be rebuilt from the ground up. The company took a hard look at the concepts of partnerships, flexibility, customization, and speed of delivery.

Levi Strauss & Co. pulled 200 people from their regular jobs and put them into dedicated teams. They weren't replaced—coworkers stepped up the pace to keep the day-to-day business running smoothly. Each team took on a single element of the supply chain and worked with retail customers to perfect it. The targets were aggressive:

- Replenish product within thirty-six hours of receipt of the order, down from several weeks or even months.
- Ship at least 90 percent of the units accurately.
- Deliver floor-ready product that will allow our customer to make it immediately available to the consumer.
- For nonreplenishable product, deliver every order at least 90 percent complete and accurate on the date requested by the customer.

"When we first presented the targets," Tom remembers, "someone said, 'What are you smoking?' And it's true—the goals we've set for ourselves essentially require us to change the tire on a car going sixty miles per hour or rewire a house with the lights on."

The difficulty of hitting such targets wasn't lost on Bob Rockey, president of Levi Strauss & Co. North America, who compared it to "playing volleyball in the middle of a hurricane with the winds of change buffeting us as we work together." But Levi Strauss & Co. had to set bold and audacious goals in order to continue its success.

A GIANT IN ITS FIELD

Ask anyone at Intel how it achieved a 600 percent increase in revenue over the last ten years and you'll hear about Moore's Law: *the performance of chip technology, as measured by price, doubles every eighteen months.* In 1965 Gordon Moore, cofounder of Intel, observed that a dollar spent today gets you twice the performance it would have a year and a half ago.

While many people back then—most notably Intel's competitors—couldn't imagine technology developing so quickly, Moore's Law turned out to be right on the money. Microchip companies all run at a breakneck pace just to stay even with one another. Industry leaders like Intel must improve at an even faster rate if they expect to stay in front. In fact, Intel moves so fast that it usually surpasses itself, much less giving competitors a chance to catch up.

For example, Intel set the stan-

> *It's immoral not to give people the tools to meet tough goals.*
>
> —STEVE KERR,
> Chief Learning
> Officer,
> General Electric

dard for the industry when it put out the revolutionary Pentium Processor. Yet just a short fourteen months later Intel leapfrogged the Pentium with its much faster Pentium Pro.

"Intel is always moving forward, even if it means eating our own children," says Keith Erickson of Intel strategic materials. Jim Zurn, senior manager of quality technology for research and development, agrees. "Around here, if you're not running, you're going to get run over."

Intel maintains its lead with a panoramic perspective and diligent attention to the job at hand. "One of our strengths is the ability to focus on what's most important right now—to make money today," explains Greg Spirakis, microprocessor product group quality and reliability manager. "But if that's all you focus on, eventually you'll look up and say, 'Oh my God, there's a cliff three feet in front of us and there's nothing we can do about it!' For our company to survive, we need to throw a dart into the future and point the company in a direction. Then you can say, 'It kinda looks like there's a cliff over here, and a mountain over there, and somebody's building a road nearby. I think we want to go this way.' And then a year goes by and the mountain was a mirage, the road looks more real, and the cliff is pushed back another year. The path will never be a straight line, but you always have to meander forward."

Greg essentially describes the planning process that enables Intel to strategize and execute simultaneously.

- **Five years out:** Senior executives speculate about the industry outlook. What fundamental changes are in store? Will there be a new class of users to target? What technologies are needed that don't currently exist?
- **Three years out:** The executive team outlines a plan to move Intel in the right direction for the next few years.
- **Current year:** Executives set three corporate objectives that become every employee's mantra—"stapled to the foreheads of everyone at Intel," as one person put it. Each department must detail its role in achieving the goals. From the departmental plan, individuals develop priorities for the year.

Each person's workload is a microcosm of the entire planning process. An employee spends roughly 10 percent of his or her time working toward the three-to-five-year vision; 20 percent goes toward the one-to-three-year plan; and the remaining 70 percent is focused on the three annual corporate objectives, which in 1995 were to ship Pentiums, make the PC the center of the universe, and get back to Intel Basics.

Intel is totally aligned—focused on short-term results and long-term possibilities. The priorities of each employee are tied directly to the department business plan, which links to the corporate objectives. The objectives in turn support the long-range vision of the company. Each year the executive team begins the cycle all over again.

Intel and Levi Strauss & Co. are making bold strides into the future. They set audacious goals when business is good and break them down into achievable elements. Both companies excel at business as usual while constantly pursuing new possibilities. They are giants, with their feet on the ground and their heads in the stars.

INSIGHT TO ACTION

Insight 3: Have the Courage to Set Bold Goals

Keep Your Feet on the Ground and Your Head in the Stars

❑ Find out what your customers' biggest dreams are for their relationships with you.

❑ Set three bold goals to make them realities.

• _____

• _____

• _____

❑ Pull together an action team of star performers to figure out how to make it happen.

❑ Ask people what tools and support they need to achieve the goals.

❑ Take care of today's business, but list two dreams you will pursue.

• _____

• _____

Practice 10

Color Outside the Lines

In The Phantom Tollbooth, *Norton Juster's celebration of learning for the child in all of us, a boy named Milo travels the Kingdom of Knowledge. Everywhere he goes, Milo learns invaluable lessons from a host of fascinating characters—including a lesson in perspective from Alec Bings at the Point of View:*

> *"From here that looks like a bucket of water," Alec said, pointing to a bucket of water, "but from an ant's point of view it's a vast ocean, from an elephant's, just a cool drink, and to a fish, of course, it's home. So, you see, the way you see things depends a great deal on where you look at them from."*

When you look at a problem from the same old point of view, you can't make the leap in thinking necessary to hit daring targets. Talk to people with fresh perspectives.

Study how other industries do business. Bring together people whose job descriptions don't relate to the issue at hand. Real breakthroughs come when you step outside your comfort zone and explore new possibilities. You will find a great ocean where before you saw only a bucket of water.

Coloring outside the lines requires you to:

- **Open your eyes to new perspectives and possibilities.**
- **Go with your gut.**
- **Let your people go for it.**

OPEN YOUR EYES TO NEW PERSPECTIVES AND POSSIBILITIES

Inner-city communities like Coliseum Gardens and Mount Hope have long suffered from "the same old point of view." Typically, "experts" arrive with a quick-fix solution for an unaccepting community. They hand over the instruction manual, then skip town. When the program of the month fails, the experts blame it on the community, who obviously didn't implement the program properly. (You may know some consultants who fit this description . . .)

"People don't like it when you try to therapize them," says Beverley Wilson. "We didn't want to do it that same old way. We told people, 'We're not coming to give you anything, you've already got everything you need.'" The

Health Realization approach works where so many others failed because everyone connected to an inner-city community learns to see through new eyes. Social workers, teachers, police officers, and even politicians are taught to see the residents of housing projects as poor people, not bad people. Likewise, residents begin to see the dreaded "authorities" as human beings who are just doing a job the best way they know how.

Beverley was teaching a class at Coliseum Gardens about the power of shedding conditioned thinking. "I said, 'Just mentally strip. Take off whatever you think you are and whatever you think I am. Just let our souls meet.' So here comes Jerry, the community police officer, walking into our meeting decked out in full uniform. He had no idea what our lesson was about that day—he just came by to check out our class. As soon as he stepped in the door, I could see this one older resident looking at him—almost fondling him with her eyes. Just a few months before, the sight of him made her furious! But she mentally stripped him of his uniform and really tried to see the person underneath. Suddenly she said, 'I can't even believe I'm going to do this, but I like you!' She hugged him! She actually hugged

> *If you are going to do something big, you should just do it. There's no stepping into the water toe by toe: it'll take you forever to get wet. If you're going to do it, just plunge in. You'll adjust to the temperature of the water much quicker.*
>
> —VICKI YOUNG,
> Director of Sales and Marketing,
> The Ritz-Carlton Tysons Corner

him! Looking at people from a new perspective is so easy. It's just like mining for gold."

New perspectives and possibilities turn hidden options into golden opportunities. Coliseum Gardens and Mount Hope are casting off the impotent solutions of a myopic point of view. Instead, the old bucket of water has become a vast ocean, and whole communities ride a new wave of hope.

GO WITH YOUR GUT

At a recent **Service/Quality Leadership Forum 2000,** Roger Mills, president of the Health Realization Institute, captivated the room with his dramatic stories about the transformation of inner-city communities. "What processes and techniques get these kinds of results?" asked an executive.

"Process and technique are poor excuses for understanding," Roger replied.

No technique, handbook, or policy manual can address the ever-changing, real-life situations we all encounter day in and day out. If you *understand* a situation, you know what is needed. Keep your bearings and trust your intuition.

> You've got to have the courage to fly in the face of conventional wisdom. A lot of people fail because they don't know what they want to be. You've got to take a stand and try some things.
>
> —DAVID POTTRUCK, President and COO, The Charles Schwab Corporation

83

TO FEE OR NOT TO FEE

Charles Schwab went with its gut and colored outside the lines, more than doubling its IRA business as a result. "Our biggest complaint was about IRA fees," says David Pottruck, president and COO of Charles Schwab Corporation:

> We charged twenty-two dollars annually to maintain an IRA account, one of the lowest prices in the market. But customers hated that fee because they didn't sense there was a service—like sitting down in a restaurant and having to pay for a menu. There was just a notion of fairness, a notion of what's right for our customers. In 1991 we launched the No-Fee IRA in a world where everybody was charging fees.
>
> It was a tough decision. It cost nothing to collect that money. Electronic debit of the account, and bang!—$9 million dollars to our bottom line. That was very painful to give up, but it had an enormous impact on the market. I had people tell me, "Getting rid of the fee for the IRA was so wonderful. My mother had an $85,000 IRA at another brokerage house, and I moved it to Schwab." And I'm thinking, you moved it to Schwab to save twenty-two dollars? It's crazy to move an $85,000 account for twenty-two! It's like saying, "I bought this car because it had a free lighter" or "The guy threw in free mats." For whatever reason, that twenty-two dollars was very meaningful to our customers. Ultimately, our competitors had to follow us.

The financials said no. The gut said yes. Charles Schwab made the right decision, and an entire industry scrambled to follow suit.

LET YOUR PEOPLE GO FOR IT

When a bold goal provides a stirring call to action, the entire organization accelerates to high speed with new optimism. Peter McIntosh, senior vice president of brokerage operations, is the maverick at Schwab who embodies the spirit of coloring outside the lines. He rallies his people around audacious targets and liberates them to get the job done.

If you want 5 percent improvement, get yourself another boy. If you want huge improvement—75 percent improvement—do it our way. We set the goal, "We will not lose one damn piece of paper." None of these Mickey Mouse targets like, "We'll reduce paper-loss by 10 percent." What is the physical limit? The physical limit is that we won't lose one damn sheet of paper. That's the target. End of analysis. No debate.

But no target date. I don't care if it happens this year or next year. Just let there be no doubt where we're going. If you say, "Do it in fifty years," people are going to take fifty years to get there. But if you don't set a date and just tell people where you want to go, you might get it done in six months. So I just say, "Get going. If you have an idea, do it."

Recently, I heard that one of the branches thought we'd lost a sheet of paper. So I called an emergency meeting. I said, "I want a meeting right now on this sheet of paper." We finally figured out that the branch had never sent it to us. In fact, the branch still had it. Case closed.

We hit seemingly impossible targets within a matter of months. My staff gets turned on by huge, gutsy targets.

Incremental change is death. I say you set huge, heroic goals, and then tell your people, "Take any steps you want, as long as it brings us closer."

Peter's bold goals are tight and uncompromising—an emergency meeting to locate one piece of paper ensures that his people know what's most important. But Peter frees his people to explore new ways to achieve them. Coloring outside the lines makes for speed, optimism, and big-time results.

INSIGHT TO ACTION

Insight 3: Have the Courage to Set Bold Goals

Color Outside the Lines

❑ Coloring outside the lines requires you to change your perspective. With your team, go to a movie, visit other companies, explore a children's art museum, go to a ball game, etc.

❑ Define three things you're not doing now that would dramatically increase profits and the satisfaction of your people and customers.

- _____

- _____

- _____

❑ Make them the main topic of conversation—seek ways to do them.

❑ Enrich every team with a few people whose day-to-day responsibilities have nothing to do with the task at hand.

❑ Create a "Strategic Surprise Team" of mavericks whose only job is to explore innovative ways to improve.

Practice 11

No Company Is an Island

Partnering and cooperation need to be our watch-words. Just like a marriage, we need to give more than we get, and believe that it will all work out better in the end.

—ROBERT NOYCE

The late Bob Noyce understood that, whether in life or in business, we can't go it alone. As co-inventor of the integrated circuit, cofounder of Intel, and the first CEO of SEMATECH, his life exemplifies what can be accomplished with bold goals and collaboration. You are surrounded by a wealth of perspectives and resources to better define and achieve your goals. Seek out critical partnerships and vital information beyond the four walls of your organization.

- **Involve customers in defining goals.** Your goals are worthless unless they are based on the needs of your customers.
- **Partner with suppliers and vendors.** They have knowledge to share about what other companies are doing and the exciting breakthroughs just around the corner. Besides, you can't achieve your goals if your suppliers can't deliver.
- **Cooperate with competitors.** Yes, you heard right. Decide which things, if done together, would benefit everyone. Compete like crazy on the rest.
- **Get everyone on board.** Make sure that everyone involved is dedicated to hitting the target.

A BOLD EXPERIMENT IN COOPERATION

From microwave ovens to communications satellites, semiconductors are vital ingredients of practically every modern electronic system. They are the technological base of America's economic strength and defense strategy. The ability to develop and competitively manufacture leading-edge designs is critical to the nation's economy and security.

But in 1987 the domestic semiconductor industry was rapidly moving offshore. The Japanese had entered the market and were slashing prices to capture market share. "We were all in a death spiral, on our way to extinction," said one industry insider, bluntly describing the situation that faced U.S. manufacturers and suppliers.

To restore world leadership in semiconductor manufacturing technology, competing U.S. semiconductor companies, along with the federal government, formed an unprecedented consortium—SEMATECH (SEmiconductor MAnufacturing TECHnology). Each member company had to contribute a small percentage of its annual profits and send a few of its best people to SEMATECH for two or three years. SEMATECH, in exchange, guaranteed a return on investment of at least three to one. Instead of individual companies investing millions of dollars exploring precompetitive processes and equipment, SEMATECH would do the research on their behalf and share the results.

Sound impossible? It almost was. The fourteen charter members of SEMATECH were fierce competitors in the marketplace. "You think there was an iron curtain across Europe? Well the iron curtain around each of these companies was even more impenetrable," remembers Bill Spencer, CEO of SEMATECH. "Getting them to work together on something of interest to all of them was a big problem. They were afraid of giving away the family jewels. For them to come together and break down those barriers was a huge step forward."

"'This is crazy! We're the leaders!'" echoed Intel's Keith Erickson. "'Why are we going in and always giving up stuff to Texas Instruments and Motorola? We have the best!' Well, we found out we didn't. In most cases we were pretty

> *Nothing is impossible for the man who doesn't have to do it himself.*
>
> —A. H. WEILER

good, but there were companies that had stuff just as good as we did—even better sometimes."

SEMATECH's immediate task was to perform "industrial triage." Semiconductor manufacturers had a strained relationship with a dwindling U.S. supplier network. They needed common standards and access to quality equipment and materials. The consortium could never rebuild an entire industry without outside support. It brought together suppliers, universities, and scientists to define the common goal—and achieve it.

SEMATECH's bold experiment in cooperation elevated each member company's level of performance—Intel, for example, went from number ten to number one in world market share. By 1992 the United States had regained global leadership in semiconductor manufacturing. SEMATECH continues, however. The member companies recognize the awesome power of collaboration—in 1995 the average return on their investment in SEMATECH was four to one. SEMATECH is phasing out government support and is eager for the next challenge—to *keep* the U.S. industry on top.

A FOUNDATION FOR THE FUTURE

The onslaught of challenges facing health care providers are as daunting as those overcome by the semiconductor industry—and make cooperation just as essential. Mid-Columbia Medical Center partners with insurance companies, suppliers, competing hospitals, and local folks to strengthen the health of the community they share. Teaming up with three other hospitals in the area, for example, reduced costs and improved the quality of care. Mid-Columbia and its partners bought one MRI unit for all to share and pooled their printing service needs. In fact, the hospitals identified over 100 areas where they can cooperate, and have saved over $350,000 to date. The savings should increase to $1.7 million by 1998.

"We're putting that savings back into our community, and it's got my blood moving," says Mark Scott. "We've identified the critical health care problems in the area and, ironically, most of those problems revolve around children—from child abuse to substance abuse to teen pregnancy. We've agreed, as a four-hospital consortium, to invest part of the money we save by collaborating and integrating in a foundation. We're using the interest income to improve the health status of children in our region. This is the stuff we ought to be doing in health care, versus duplicating technology and trying to strategize how to kick the hell out of the guy down the street."

There's no limit to the bold goals you can achieve when you get off your island and start testing the waters around you. What could a similar collaborative effort do for education, community services, and your industry?

INSIGHT TO ACTION

Insight 3: Have the Courage to Set Bold Goals

No Company Is an Island

❑ Collaborate with a supplier on one area to improve both your businesses.

❑ Bring together local businesses, government, and education. Identify a major problem facing your community and work together to improve it.

❑ If you dare, define one (legal) opportunity on which to collaborate with your competitors for mutual benefit.

ENTHUSIASTIC
CUSTOMERS

INSPIRED
PEOPLE

FINANCIAL
PERFORMANCE

8. Lead with Care

7. Unleash the Power of People

6. Measure Well, Act Fast

5. Make Technology Your Servant

4. Simplify, Simplify, Simplify

3. Have the Courage to Set Bold Goals

2. Make Every Customer Feel Special

1. Build a Strong Foundation

Insight 4

Simplify, Simplify, Simplify

Can you imagine teaching people to ski when they've never seen snow? Marriott took on a similar challenge when it built a hotel in Warsaw, Poland. In a country where service had been abysmal throughout forty years of Communist rule, the company found an innovative way to train new hires to provide first-class service.

Marriott decided to hire people with great attitudes and bring them to the United States to experience preeminent service for themselves. The Polish management trainees worked in Marriott hotels around the United States for two months, mastering the positions they would supervise at the Warsaw Marriott.

The team returned to Poland to conduct a two-week training course for newly hired associates. The afternoon of the first day of training, the general manager saw the bell captain walking around the lobby and asked why he wasn't training his staff.

"We finished at lunchtime, so I let everyone go home," the bell captain explained. "Don't worry, my team will be ready for opening day."

When the hotel opened, the bellmen received rave reviews for their outstanding service. The general manager asked the bell captain to share his training secrets at a staff meeting.

"My people aren't stupid," said the bell captain. "I got my staff together and for about two hours I told them what I'd observed in the United States. Then I reached into my pocket and pulled out the wad of money I earned in my two months there. I told them, 'If you do a phenomenal job, really hustle, and give people great service with a smile, they will give you this. And you get to keep it.' The rest is fine-tuning."

RECAPTURE CLARITY AND SIMPLICITY

Nothing is more effective than simplicity. The Polish bell captain didn't need to give two weeks of mind-numbing training. His people didn't memorize Regulation 65A from page 90 of the employee handbook. The bell captain's message was clear—make customers happy and you will make more money. That was his top priority, that was his process, and that was the end result.

The Lord's Prayer is 66 words long. The Gettysburg Address has 286 words. There are 1,332 words in the

Declaration of Independence. The 1995 United States government regulations on the sale of cabbage total 26,911 words.

Gary Fields, president of Merge Technologies in Napa, just got a notice from Newark Electronics that begins, "We are currently developing procedures to facilitate a more effective application of your cash remittances." Oh shuddup. How about "We are about to make it easier for you to pay your bills"?

—San Francisco Chronicle

Our world and our lives have become very complex. The paperwork empire rises. Bureaucracy tightens its chokehold on clarity and simplicity. Market leaders of the future will master the art of making the complex simple by reclaiming an era when craftsmen learned by doing; priorities were clear, simple, and few; and people spoke plainly and honestly.

Simplicity liberates people, enthuses customers, and increases efficiency. Set yourself apart from the competition—recapture the wisdom of the Polish bell captain and be the easiest organization to do business with in your industry.

Practice 12 **MAKE PRIORITIES MEMORABLE AND FEW**

Practice 13 **DON'T MAKE CUSTOMERS JUMP THROUGH HOOPS**

Practice 14 **NEVER CONFUSE PAPER TRAILS WITH TRAILBLAZING**

Practice 12

Make Priorities Memorable and Few

Our life is frittered away by detail. . . . Simplify, simplify.

—HENRY DAVID THOREAU,
Walden

When Sue consults with a company she talks to senior management and line employees right off the bat. "Typically, senior management is frustrated because the organization isn't working on the four corporate objectives they set. Employees are frustrated as well, because each corporate objective has seven subpoints. The company is kidding itself—in reality it's struggling to go twenty-eight directions at once." Although it may jeopardize the vitality of the laminated card industry, make priorities memorable and few.

- **Minimize priorities to maximize results.** TARP studies show that senior management can't effectively drive more than three strategic priorities at once.
- **All investments do not perform equally.** You know you're in trouble if you find a total quality management team debating where to move the water cooler. TARP recommends identifying then attacking the three key "points of pain"—areas that pose the biggest threats to employee satisfaction, customer enthusiasm, and your bottom line.
- **Liberate people to make decisions.** Every individual must understand how his or her specific job supports the few strategic priorities. When the objectives are clear and meaningful, people make the right decisions and move much faster.

INTEL INSIDER

Intel demands incredible discipline with regard to its three annual corporate objectives, then lets its people go. "As Intel grows and cycle times get reduced, we don't have time to micromanage anybody," says Keith Erickson. "Basically, everyone is automatically empowered. I've had people in my organization reorganize their work teams without even asking me. They know where the company is going and what their role is, so they take the risks and do what's right."

Details on how the workforce stays focused came from

another Intel insider—Eli, our research assistant's fourth-grade friend. She asked how school was going and he retorted, "I'm not a student, I work for Intel!" His class received a grant from Intel and is learning some Intel techniques. Students don't have homework, they have "ARs," or Action Requireds. They hold a weekly "BUM," or Business Update Meeting, where each student-employee shares three things: What did I learn this week? What will I learn next week? What problems am I having?

People at Intel discuss progress toward the three corporate objectives in the same way: What did I do this week? What will I do next week? What problems am I having? It's charming to see fourth graders huddled in a Business Update Meeting, but for Intel it's a serious way to keep a highly empowered workforce focused on the vital few priorities. If you are interested in hiring our fourth-grade friend as a consultant to help clarify your priorities, look him up at http://www.ar.bum.com.

NOTHING HAPPENS IF SOMEBODY DOESN'T SELL SOMETHING

Mary Kay Cosmetics has one strategic priority: meet the needs of the sales force. "Nothing happens if somebody doesn't sell something," explains President Larry Harley. "Our universe revolves around the sales force. Anything we do has to pass the test: Is it good for the sales force? Does this help them? Is this what they want? Does this add value to them? If that's the case, then we proceed. I mean, they're the ones we bet our lives on. The sales force sends my kids to college—I bet my life on those people."

ONE HOTEL, ONE PERSON AT A TIME

When The Ritz-Carlton announced it was competing for the Malcolm-Baldrige National Quality Award, previous winners and long-time applicants laughed. The company had only eighteen months to elevate every aspect of its business to a world-class level. But The Ritz-Carlton had a plan—get there thirty-three times faster by having each of its thirty-three hotels perfect one aspect of the business. The San Francisco property, for example, improved the company's hiring process. Another hotel streamlined housekeeping procedures. After building extraordinary competence in a single area, each property shared its results.

> *Be master of your petty annoyances and conserve your energies for the big worthwhile things. It isn't the mountain ahead that wears you out—it's the grain of sand in your shoe.*
>
> —ROBERT SERVICE

Eighteen months later, The Ritz-Carlton Hotel Company accepted the Malcolm-Baldrige National Quality Award from the President of the United States. The prizewinning process continues to build expertise and a worldwide strategic advantage for the luxury hotel chain.

People work best when they have a few memorable objectives to pursue. Horst Schulze personally ensures that The Ritz-Carlton's corporate objectives are meaningful to employees from Singapore to Atlanta. "When a new hotel opens, I meet with the staff individually to discuss where we need to go as a company. I sit down with the dishwasher and say, 'Here are our corporate objectives. What is your role in relation to them? What do you want to achieve? Where do you want to be six months from now?' And he tells me. Right then I say, 'Okay, this is your purpose in coming to work. It's up to you how you want to accomplish it.' I make sure each person knows how to contribute to the company. Since individual objectives are written sitting down with me in blue jeans, they are personal and meaningful. People can no longer refer to the company as 'they' or 'them.' It is 'me.'"

The Ritz-Carlton minimizes priorities, charging each hotel with a specific area to improve, and makes corporate priorities memorable for its people. The company maximizes results—J.D. Power and Associates reports that The Ritz-Carlton is far and away the preference leader in the luxury hotel segment.

In a crowd of competitors struggling with a million priorities, Intel, The Ritz-Carlton, and Mary Kay Cosmetics stand out. Each narrows its priorities down to a handful. Their people have a solid understanding of what needs to be done and use their creativity and wisdom to achieve it.

INSIGHT TO ACTION

Insight 4: Simplify, Simplify, Simplify

Make Priorities Memorable and Few

❏ Rank your priorities, then kill a few.

❏ Perform a reality check on how well the top three priorities of senior management, staff, and customers are aligned.

Senior Management	Staff	Customers
_____	_____	_____
_____	_____	_____
_____	_____	_____

❏ Have people make each decision pass a litmus test: Is this good for our people, customers, and profits?

❏ If it's good for:

- All three—just do it!
- For two and not the other—let's talk.
- For one and not the other two—probably not.

Practice 13

Don't Make Customers Jump through Hoops

One chic restaurant in Washington, D.C., made head-lines: "Man Thrown Out for Ordering Risotto." A patron saw that risotto was served as an entrée and asked for a small portion as an appetizer. The waiter went back to check with the chef, who owned the estab-lishment. He returned shortly. "I'm sorry, we do not serve risotto as an appetizer."

"Fine, I'll pay the whole entrée price, but please bring it first as my appetizer."

"I'm afraid you don't understand, sir. We do not serve risotto as an appetizer."

"This is crazy! I just want risotto!"

The chef came out of the kitchen. "Risotto is not meant to be an appetizer," he said coldly. "It must be a main course. And you, sir, must leave my restaurant."

The incredulous patron refused to leave. The police were called in, and the unfortunate fellow was escorted from the premises for ordering risotto as an appetizer.

Don't make customers jump through hoops—simplify the customer experience. Levi Strauss & Co. gets you the jeans you want. USAA tracks your feedback twenty-four hours a day. Marriott gets you checked in faster. When customers order the equivalent of risotto as an appetizer in your business, what are the odds they'll get it hassle-free? Be incredibly convenient. Your customers will thank you—in dollars and loyalty.

ORDER FROM CHAOS

Like Mid-Columbia Medical Center, Harbor Hospital in South Baltimore, Maryland, delivers care the way patients want it. The philosophy of the inner-city hospital puts the needs and values of the person in the hospital bed at the center of the universe. Harbor breaks down the complexity of traditional hospitals to make the customer experience as easy as possible.

Everyone dreads hospital admitting rooms—a frightening, chaotic mass of people suffering from every ailment imaginable. Why do hospitals care more about your insurance company than about you? At Harbor it's no longer necessary—or acceptable—for sick people to sit in the lobby waiting for someone to ask them the name of their insurance company. Harbor decentralizes the admissions process. The hospital admits patients on any patient floor or even bedside and cuts the normal processing time in half.

Robin Orr, former executive director of the Planetree Organization and a leading health care consultant, helped both Harbor and Mid-Columbia implement their patient-centered transformation. "No wonder patients feel like no one really cares about them. They face a never-ending parade of fifty to sixty people a day coming in and out of their room. At Harbor, every patient is assigned a 'Care Pair'—a registered nurse and a clinical associate who are the primary caregivers. Patients establish a personal relationship with their Care Pair and feel truly cared for."

> *As soon as you are complicated, you are ineffectual.*
> —KONRAD ADENAUER

Patients also receive a case manager who tracks the healing process and coordinates home care with the family. When patients leave the hospital, the case manager provides educational materials, sets up future appointments, and follows up with phone calls once they get home.

THANKS FOR THE INFORMATION

We're all intimidated by the hospital environment and feel helpless faced with the complete lack of information. Mid-Columbia's Health Resource Center solves both problems. "We located the Resource Center right downtown," explains Michele Spatz, director of Mid-Columbia's Planetree Health Resource Center. "We didn't want it in the hospital because people aren't comfortable visiting the hospital. We wanted to make it a homey, comfortable, and safe environment, so we're located in a remodeled Victorian home." People can relax and learn in a distinctively un-hospital-like environment. The books, magazines, and videos are easy to use and organized by anatomy, diagnosis, and treatment. Everything is in plain English.

> *A leader's job is to make the complex simple.*
>
> —BILL COONEY, President, Property and Casualty Insurance, USAA

Wouldn't you be delighted if you went to a department store and had one person to help you through the entire experience? What if the case manager from your local computer store called two days after you brought home your PC—just to see if you had questions or problems? Patients certainly aren't the only customers who appreciate ease, convenience, and personal attention. If you created case managers in your business, what would they do?

INCREDIBLY CONVENIENT

Sue went to Saks Fifth Avenue to buy a coat for an upcoming business trip.

I was thrilled to find the perfect coat. As I paid for it, the salesperson assured me it would be altered in time for my trip three days later. The day arrived, and I double-parked on the way to the airport to pick up my coat. They couldn't find it in the coat department and dispatched me to alterations. A seamstress finally brought out my coat and it fit great. I thanked her and headed for the door—but she stopped me.

"You can't take it like that—we have to get a special coat bag from the coat department." I said that wouldn't be necessary, but she said it wasn't an option—store policy dictated that all coats must be hung and bagged by the coat department. I couldn't take it anymore. Coat in hand, I dashed for the escalator and out the door to my waiting car.

A simple purchase became a hellish experience because the staff refused to alter rigid policies. Customers don't care about coat bags, they care about positive, hassle-free transactions.

Contrast this experience to one Sue had at The Ritz-Carlton Hotel in Atlanta. "Once again, I was late for my flight and had to check out quickly. The desk clerk went to another counter, completed the transaction, and returned. I suddenly realized I was standing at the concierge desk. I apologized and offered to move over, but the clerk said, 'Don't be silly, Ms. Cook, you can check out anywhere you like!' I was blown away that the clerk altered his service to make my check-out easier."

Sometimes you have to bend the rules—or even throw them out—to do what's right for the customer. As Kenny Rogers sang in "The Gambler," "Know when to hold them, know when to fold them."

INSIGHT TO ACTION

Insight 4: Simplify, Simplify, Simplify

Don't Make Customers Jump through Hoops

❑ Find two areas where you've got customers jumping through hoops and eliminate them.

- _____

- _____

❑ Ask customers what conveniences they value most. List the top three and make them priorities.

- _____

- _____

- _____

❑ Have teams map out the internal steps for delivering your products and services. Take out unnecessary steps and redundancies.

Insight 4: Simplify, Simplify, Simplify

Practice 14

Never Confuse Paper Trails with Trailblazing

Bureaucracies, systems, and regulations are necessary only if you believe that people are either stupid or evil.

—MICHELE HUNT

Michele Hunt left her job as vice president for people at Herman Miller to do something a little more challenging— simplify the federal government. She was appointed by President Clinton to head up the Federal Quality Institute, charged with introducing words like *customer, simplicity,* and *efficiency* to the various agencies of the U.S. government. The Federal Quality Institute gathered the greatest minds in the private sector to coach agencies like NASA and the IRS. It reoriented the Department of Education on the needs of its customer—the student/learner. It helped

110

U.S. Customs transform itself, getting rid of forty-five district and seven regional offices. Customs employees were deployed to the ports, closer to their customers. You may have experienced the result—a drastic reduction in time spent going through customs.

"The federal government is the closest thing I can imagine to institutional slavery," says Michele. "The rules, regulations, and systems bind people so tightly they end up working to serve the system itself instead of the American people. But government bureaucracy is just an extreme form of what exists in corporations all across America."

Whether a small partnership or the federal government, any organization must tear down the barriers preventing people from getting work done. Unfortunately, when companies talk about "being easy," they only think about simplifying the customer experience. But how much paperwork, redundancy, and procedure do your people need to fight through to serve the customer?

Make work easy by simplifying processes, communications, and the chain of command. Cut down on paperwork and meetings. Create systems that serve people instead of enslaving them.

Simplify your business internally as well as externally to:

- **save time and money.**
- **enable people to work more effectively.**
- **reduce turnover of people and customers.**
- **develop new products and services more quickly.**
- **spend more time building enthusiastic customers.**

111

THE ULTIMATE SYSTEMS BUSTER

Peter McIntosh of Charles Schwab is the ultimate systems buster. He disintegrates the barriers that prevent his people from doing their jobs the best way they can.

"I *hate* unnecessary paper," says Peter:

I recently had to write four or five pages on something, and it took me hours making it look pretty and everything. I was furious! That is downtime where I didn't get to talk to my branches and I didn't get to talk to my staff. Oh, and meetings—there's just too many. Meetings and paper are a deadly combination. People sitting around reading paper! Not even talking! Paper stifles the organization, plain and simple. So I've sort of forbidden paper for internal communication.

The other big one of mine is, "You touch it, you own it." Simple problems should have simple solutions—don't pass them off. If it looks like something wrong is going on, there used to be nothing we could do. Our back office people weren't allowed to call the customer directly because we didn't have "customer service training." That's ridiculous! My staff members break that rule and do what's right. "Mr. Smith, I understand you want to do thus and so." He says, "Yes, I do." My guy says, "You know that if you do this the IRS will take all your worldly possessions?" "Oh, it will?" "Yes, but if you do it slightly different, you'll be just fine." "Oh really, well thank you for the advice. Thank you very much." That took a lot of customer service training, right? In every organization there are crazy rules and systems like this creating barriers for people.

We're changing a lot of systems and procedures here. Some

people say, "Oh my God, they're changing procedures at the same time as they're changing systems! Stop! We can't change procedures until we discover the exact ramifications for the systems—or else we'll have chaos!"

Well, you know what that means—a bunch of long planning meetings, a bunch of paper, and a bunch of analysis. What I say is, "Staff, this is where I want to go, so let's start doing lots of stuff to get there." We need systems anyway. We need procedures anyway. If we try to figure out which to do first and what their exact form should be, we'll be analyzing for the next five years, in which case I could've done two generations of both. Remember, people want to go fast. They want to change and move. They hate endless analysis of little things—it knocks the wind out of them.

Of course there is potential for mistakes, and that's fine. In fact, my goal is to implement flawed systems. Think of the alternative! Endlessly contemplating what would be perfect! Analysis takes the place of optimism—the fundamental belief that you can do great things with the people you've got. If you want something big, you have to assume you're going to get it and just do it.

Peter's tenacity has virtually eliminated memos and white papers in brokerage operations. Decisions are made on the spot, because when people touch a problem, they own it. Now that problems are fixed immediately, Schwab's "reject rate"—problematic paperwork that must be redone—has shrunk from 25 percent to 4 percent. But Peter isn't the only one with an eye for simplicity. Everyone at Schwab is encouraged to streamline. The message is clear: If it doesn't add value, eliminate it.

HUDDLE UP AND CALL THE PLAY

Every Ritz-Carlton hotel worldwide holds a daily line-up meeting where critical information is shared and immediately put to practical use. Before every shift, each department huddles for ten minutes. Each person receives a small packet with the day's vital information—projected hotel occupancy, a list of VIP guests and their preferences, special conference and meeting needs, and The Ritz-Carlton basic principle of the day. The daily line-up meeting ensures that people begin work armed with their marching orders, keeps everyone in touch with the business, and builds consistency. This simple face-to-face meeting enables The Ritz-Carlton to communicate anything to every employee in one day. This is a proven idea you can implement in ten minutes to improve your communications tenfold.

GET YOURSELF CONNECTED

Is your desk overflowing with paperwork? Do you spend half the day in meetings? Are your voice mail and e-mail filled with irrelevant messages? Paperwork and meetings *must* be the best way to communicate, because our experience shows they consume 70 percent of the typical organization's time. But no data says paperwork and meetings are the most effective ways to get things done. In fact, ask about their effectiveness and the phrases "couldn't care less" and "waste of time" come up an awful lot. On the other hand, a rumor spreads through an entire organization in no time flat—and gets everyone interested and excited.

"Corporate programs that rely on meetings and memos fail because they address the formal, structured organization and don't capture people's hearts and minds," says John Seely Brown, chief scientist at Xerox. "We're designing communications systems and ways of working that maximize the speed and excitement of the human side of the organization."

> *Implementing a good plan now is better than implementing a perfect plan next week.*
>
> —GENERAL GEORGE PATTON

At Xerox, structuring work the way people actually communicate and learn makes it easier and more meaningful. The company's copier repairmen, for example, had standard-issue manuals on how to fix every problem a copier could have, but they weren't carrying the manuals with them on repairs. "The repairmen said the manuals were too heavy and were written so badly they couldn't understand them anyway," explains John.

Xerox experimented with a new approach. The company gave the repairmen two-way radios with an open channel, enabling them to talk to each other on the job. They talked about sports, hobbies, their families, and company gossip, but they also discussed how to fix things. One repairman would ask, "Anybody know what to do when tray 4 is jamming?" and a fellow technician would offer suggestions. "I just saw that yesterday. Wire A to B and . . ."

115

Just like a rumor, knowledge traveled fast. The know-how of one was quickly available to all. The repairmen were much happier with their work and did a better job fixing copiers. When the experiment ended, they offered to use their own money to buy the two-way radios in order to stay connected.

With only a small investment in readily available technology, work became easy and engaging. Xerox is moving away from cumbersome corporate manuals. Instead, John leads the charge to simplify systems and let people talk and work naturally.

Challenge your basic assumptions about people, work, and communications. Liberate people from stupid rules, regulations, and barriers. Once you've Turned On your people, you'll never want to go back.

INSIGHT TO ACTION

Insight 4: Simplify, Simplify, Simplify

Never Confuse Paper Trails with Trailblazing

❑ Ask people what paperwork, meetings, and systems are in their way, then vigorously eliminate them.

❑ Eliminate 50 percent of all meetings and paperwork. Hold remaining meetings in half the time.

❑ Next time you have the urge to write a memo, put your pen down (or turn off your computer), push back your chair, and go talk to the person. If you must write a memo, do it in one page.

ENTHUSIASTIC
CUSTOMERS

INSPIRED
PEOPLE

FINANCIAL
PERFORMANCE

8. Lead with Care

7. Unleash the Power of People

6. Measure Well, Act Fast

5. Make Technology Your Servant

4. Simplify, Simplify, Simplify

3. Have the Courage to Set Bold Goals

2. Make Every Customer Feel Special

1. Build a Strong Foundation

Insight 5

Make Technology Your Servant

In 1986 Roger received a letter from a businesswoman who stayed at the same Marriott hotel fifteen times that year, spending seventy-five dollars a night. Yet every time she returned to the hotel she was treated like a first-time guest. She was surprised that an organization that prided itself on service didn't even know its best customers and their unique needs. Roger went down to the people in information systems and showed them the letter.

"What can we do about this?" I asked. "It's critical to know who our best customers are so we can tailor our services to them." They got back to me a few days later and said it would cost slightly more than the national debt and take about ten years to develop.

The next week I was at our hotel in Irvine,

California, a property that I had personally been to over ten times. Bill, the doorman, took my bag, walked me to the front desk, and introduced me to the woman working there. Bill said, "This is Mr. Dow," and she looked up with a great big smile, shook my hand, and said, "Hello, Mr. Dow. It's great to have you back with us again. How was your trip?" I apologized for not remembering her and asked when we had met.

"Oh we've never met," she replied. "I just started working here two weeks ago."

"Then how do you know I've stayed here before?" I asked. She paused, but Bill jumped in. "He's with Marriott, you can tell him."

"Well," she said, "when Bill takes your bag, he asks your name and whether you've stayed with us before. If you answer 'Yes,' then when he introduces you to me, he pulls on his ear like this." She pulled on her ear-lobe. "Watch this," she said. She called over a bellman, pulled her ear, and said, "This is Mr. Dow. He'll be staying on our Concierge level."

"Hey buddy, welcome back!" said the bellman. "Let's go to your room."

Today, ten years later, Marriott has automated the ear pull. The company has one of the industry's best customer recognition programs—a system that tracks each guest's frequency, level of spending, room preference, travel patterns, and favorite hotels. Customers can no longer complain about Marriott's not knowing them. The company tailors its marketing programs for individual customers. And now, if a frequent guest stops staying with Marriott, the system alerts the company and generates a letter inviting the guest back. The associates at each hotel have detailed customer information at their fingertips, enabling them to provide personal service and take special care of their best customers. Marriott is currently building the capability to share data among each of its lodging brands.

BACK TO THE FUTURE

Technology is most effective as an enabler for a clear purpose. Marriott's purpose was always clear—to know its best customers and provide them with personal service. Ten years ago, with only 150 hotels, a low-tech solution was effective. But more than 900 hotels later, ear pulls had to be upgraded. Technology is usually thought of as complicated science, but in fact it's any tool, high- or low-tech, used to get the job done.

Customers don't care about the technology used to meet their needs. They care that you know their name and recognize how much business they give you. They want you to be accessible, efficient, and highly responsive. Make technology your servant—use it to enthuse your customers simply and cost-effectively.

"Business people don't need to know technical details about information systems—the bits, bytes, and baud

121

rates," says Regis McKenna, chairman of Gemini-McKenna, author, and technology venture capitalist. "But they must develop a business understanding of technology and how to use it strategically. Many companies blindly throw technology at every problem. What happens? Customers and people are frustrated, productivity goes down, and cost goes up. But a company totally focused on personal relationships develops useful technology naturally. It says, 'I wish I could do *this* for my customers,' then seeks the best tools for people to make it happen—tools that liberate people to work better, faster, and more creatively."

Jerry Williams, a community police officer in Coliseum Gardens, agrees that the use of technology must be people- and results-driven: "Police used to walk the beat. They knew everyone in the community and all of their problems. Then cops got fancy technology in the form of squad cars and little toys like radios, and they stayed locked in their cars all the time. You've got to be careful not to let technology separate people—it should bring them closer together."

Fifteen years ago it was easy to tell if a company invested heavily in technology—it cranked out interchangeable products and cookie-cutter service. Only businesses like cabinetmakers and corner grocers that kept their bookkeeping in milk crates offered tailored service and personal relationships.

Today companies can deliver solutions that look and feel personal to millions of customers, using simple technological systems. In fact, with the strategic use of information and database technology, any organization can re-create the personal conversations that occurred between shopkeeper and customer. "It used to be when a customer asked for a product, he knew who would be making it," says Regis. "Communication was constant and instantaneous. If the customer didn't like what he got, he marched right back to talk with the craftsman. Today's networking and information technologies enable companies to recapture the relationships and customization of yesterday."

One Saturday, Roger was at the Denver City Marriott and needed to get a package to San Francisco by Monday. "I called the Federal Express 800 number and said I'd take it to the airport if I had to. The woman on the phone replied, 'That won't be necessary. We have an office two blocks from your hotel at 1719 Glenarm Place in the Arcadia Towers building, just past the barbershop. It's open from eleven to four today.'

"I was amazed at the level of detail she had at her fingertips and told her so. 'I've never even been to Denver,' she laughed, 'but people always think I must be just a few blocks away because of the specific directions I give them on the spot. I just have a good system!'"

Federal Express feels like part of the neighborhood because it uses technology to offer customers truly personal service.

Technology, done right, creates a future that rekindles the spirit and values of the past. According to the following excerpt from *The Official America Online Membership Kit and Tour Guide* by Tom Lichty, America Online is more than network technology:

> [It's] also a community. I compare AOL to the small Oregon town where I live. People are friendly here. They say hello when they pass you on the street, they invite you to their house for a chat, and they go out of their way to be of assistance. AOL does all these things: "instant messages" allow people who are on-line at the same time to say hello and hold "passing on the street" conversations; chat rooms are electronic "rooms"—public or private—where groups of members hold real-time conversations about subjects of their choosing; and "members helping members" is a message board where members help one another with questions . . .

Open up lines of interactive communication with your customers and use that information in innovative, cost-effective ways. Make technology your servant to build personal relationships and financial performance. Your long-term vitality depends on it.

Practice 15 **LIVE A LIFE OF ACCESS**

Practice 16 **INFORMATION UPGRADE 5.0**

Practice 17 **HIT A GRAND SLAM**

Practice 15

Live a Life of Access

We get 500 channels directly from a satellite. We can have the finest lingerie from Paris overnighted to our doorstep and gourmet meals from three different restaurants delivered within the hour. We live in a world of instant gratification—and what we want is access.

Have you ever called a high-tech company expecting state-of-the-art customer service and found instead a maze of automated choices, none of which related to your question? Or been told how valuable your call is and please wait twenty-five minutes for the next available representative? Hanging up and calling back is pointless—you just have to do it all over again. Nothing is more frustrating than being denied access to a company.

People want to reach you day and night, weekends and holidays; by phone, fax, e-mail, and on the Internet; from cars, planes, hotels, home, and office. The strategic use of technology makes it all happen.

- **Put access directly into the hands of the customer.** Federal Express provides an 800 number for assistance in tracking packages. But FedEx uses innovative technology to offer customers even more direct points of entry to its business. Corporate customers receive specially designed software and computer terminals allowing them to track shipments themselves. Individuals can do the same over the Internet.

- **Beware of shattered expectations.** When Lucy holds the football for Charlie Brown to kick, she always pulls it away at the last second. Everyone sympathizes with Charlie Brown as he goes flying through the air. "Once companies open themselves up to customers," says Regis McKenna, "they must have the systems, processes, and people in place to fully support the interactions. Access raises the stakes in the company's relationships with its customers. Shattered expectations will do more harm to the relationship than not providing access at all." Charlie Brown comes back—your customers won't.

THERE'S NO PLACE LIKE HOME

When interest rates recently dropped to their lowest point in years, homeowners scrambled to refinance. You may have tried yourself, or heard horror stories about jammed lines and waiting on hold forever to talk to the bank.

Late one night Roger called the 800 number for NationsBank, which held his mortgage. "I expected to leave a message and get my name on a waiting list to be called back. I was surprised when the bank's voice-response system asked if I was interested in refinancing. The system prompted me to punch in the amount of my existing loan and monthly payment. I could even choose between a fixed or adjustable rate, and a fifteen- or thirty-year term. Then the voice said, 'At today's interest rate, your payment would be such and such. Press "1" if you would like a representative to call you. Press "2" to begin again.' A representative called the very next day, and she was ready to meet my needs. I quickly finalized the refinance of my home."

Every bank provides an 800 number, but NationsBank backs it up with direct access to its computer system twenty-four hours a day. How can you connect customers directly to your service?

100 PERCENT RELIABLE CUSTOMER SERVICE

Sales have been flat in the office furniture industry for the past five years thanks to corporate downsizing. But during that time, Miller SQA, a Herman Miller subsidiary, grew its sales and profits a phenomenal 35 percent per year. The company accomplished this feat by providing simple, quick, and affordable (SQA) furniture and executing a strategy of operational excellence. To achieve its goal of "100 percent reliable customer service," Miller SQA developed a unique technology.

Before Miller SQA came on the scene, purchasing office furniture was anything but direct. Customers flipped through a catalog and selected the pieces they wanted. They retained costly interior designers to draw up floorplans. The back-and-forth process took up to six weeks, and when customers finally placed the order, it took eight weeks more to receive the goods.

Miller SQA revolutionized the industry by providing customers with direct interactive access to its business. "Our basic insight was that the furniture buying process was a hassle," explains Gary VanSpronsen, vice president of market development. "Our solution applies technology to enable customers to 'try on' their furniture before they buy."

Like FedEx, Miller SQA gives customers a software program and a computer. The software, called Z-AXIS, is a 3-D office visualization system that combines furniture design, layout, and ordering in one easy-to-use format. "The Z-AXIS system uses a 'point and click' interface that makes designing furniture layouts as easy as playing a video game—and just as much fun," says Gary. "Our system is perfect for customers who aren't accustomed to looking at blueprints and visualizing how their offices will look. They want to see pictures. Z-AXIS allows them to plan their space and see a color 3-D picture of their future office in just minutes." What would your customers like to "try on" before they buy?

Customers of Miller SQA use the software to view from any angle exactly what their offices would look like with new furniture, reconfiguring layouts or changing variables at the click of a mouse. They can print out floorplans in 3-D and color, along with an installation plan and a complete list of materials. When a selection is made, Z-AXIS automatically orders the correct components and determines a delivery schedule via direct link with the factory. A customer acknowledgment is sent within minutes to verify the order, price, and delivery schedule.

"Our market is primarily small businesses with fewer than twenty-five offices," says Gary. "These customers look for products that are easy to order, readily available, and affordably priced, because they're used to turning on a dime. With Z-AXIS, we move faster than our customers."

Since providing customers a direct link to the factory, the ordering process runs smoother than ever. Mistakes resulting from incorrectly specified orders have been totally eliminated. In an industry where it takes eight weeks for office furniture to arrive, Miller SQA gets it to your doorstep in about three—and a special *one-week* service is available.

SCHWAB REVOLVES ON ITS ACCESS

Many deep-discount brokers charge a slightly lower price than Charles Schwab, but provide almost no service.

Many Wall Street firms gain assets the "old-fashioned way"—commission brokers to "sell" clients into buying as much as possible as often as possible. Schwab is a completely different breed of brokerage firm. It doesn't skimp on service or pressure clients. The company blazes a new trail, employing technology to give its customers the best access *and* the best service in the industry.

Schwab's high-tech, high-service approach is winning over the staunchest of Wall Street customers. "We have all types of customers," explains Susanne Lyons, senior vice president of the Active Trader segment. "Some love electronics and do almost all of their business with us electronically. They don't care to ever talk to a human being. Others want to talk to a live person before they make any move. Having many different ways to reach us is critically important."

Schwab constantly develops new technologies to bring people even closer to the information and services it provides. Some of the company's innovations include:

- Twenty-four-hour, seven-days-a-week order entry for stock trades.
- TeleBroker, which allows customers to do trades themselves by touch-tone phone—in four different languages.
- SchwabLink and StreetSmart software, which made Schwab the first brokerage firm to enable customers to trade on a home computer.
- CustomBroker, which alerts active traders to specific, real-time market information via phone, fax, or pager.

When it comes to putting access directly into the hands of customers, every brokerage firm follows Schwab's lead.

Charles Schwab and Miller SQA use technology to open lines of communication with customers. They back it up with the right systems, people, and processes to give their customers superior service every time.

INSIGHT TO ACTION

Insight 5: Make Technology Your Servant

Live a Life of Access

❑ What low-tech solutions (i.e., ear pulls) could you use every day?

❑ Insist that customers, staff, and suppliers have access to an 800 number for information and feedback twenty-four hours a day, seven days a week.

❑ How many points of access do you provide? Add one more way for your customers to reach you.

❑ Identify one area where technology could build stronger personal relationships with your customers. Go for it.

Practice 16

Information Upgrade 5.0

The watchwords used to be location, location, location. Today they're database, database, database.

—TOM PETERS

When you give your customers direct access to your company, you tap into an endless source of information. Every service experience you provide, whether over the counter or over the phone, is a golden opportunity to track customer feedback.

Regis McKenna once dialed the 800 number printed on a box of Kellogg's cereal to learn whether the company took advantage of his call. "The rep had nutritional information, just to be helpful, but didn't track my feedback," says Regis. "Kellogg's isn't taking the next step. Reps could say, 'By the way, we'd like to get your opinion on our new products. We'll send you a box of Cocoa Nuts to try. Tell us if you like them or not, and why.' Kellogg's could turn that 800 number into more than just a helpful service. It would become a strategic asset—a way to build intimate relationships and a tool to improve its business."

Phone calls, letters, e-mail, and computer transactions are perfect opportunities to involve customers and build relationships. Most companies already have these points of access in place, but don't take full advantage of them. Gather customer feedback—positive, negative, everything you can get your hands on—and use technology and information systems to turn that knowledge into personal relationships and new and improved ways of doing business.

ENSURING SUCCESS

Is your organization drowning in data? Most companies are experts at gathering information, evidenced by box after box of surveys in a back room, but find implementation difficult. "If you're not careful," warns Tim Timmerman, in charge of associate and customer feedback at USAA, "technology will provide you tons and tons of data, but not a lot of useful information that helps you make good decisions about the products and services your customers want."

USAA gathers information with the best of them, but never loses sight of its goal—a personal relationship with 2.6 million customers.

"Normally, companies gather lots of customer information, dump it in a centralized place, and then spend years charting and analyzing," says Tim. "What if we could use technology to turn the paradigm around? What if we could solve problems when we hear about them, *then* count, analyze, and fix long-term?

Our ECHO system—Every Contact Has Opportunity—does exactly that. It captures comments from our customers and people and turns that data into usable information so we can fix problems right away."

> Key point for using new technologies: Help people to do what they would have done, if they had known they could have done it.
>
> —DANIEL BURRIS, *Technotrends*

For example, a representative in the insurance department is speaking with a customer who says, "I called the USAA bank department yesterday, and Sally wasn't very helpful." The rep clicks the ECHO icon on his screen and selects the type of problem, in this case "service." Another screen pops up listing the different departments at USAA, and the rep clicks on "bank." The rep then types in the pertinent information and hits "send." Thirty seconds after the rep first heard the complaint, a message is tagged to the customer's file and sent either to Sally or to the action agent at the bank, whose job is to respond immediately.

Only after taking immediate action does USAA send information to its centralized "clearinghouse" to be analyzed. Feedback, customer surveys, customer research, and even executive correspondence is combined and assessed for long-term trends and solutions. USAA captures about 2,000 pieces of customer feedback a week with its ECHO system, enabling the company to keep a finger on the pulse of its members' changing needs. "We're so close to our customers we anticipate their needs," says Tim. "We create the *exact* products and services they want."

The ECHO system already transforms every customer contact into a business advantage, but USAA never stops looking for ways to serve its customers better. The continuous stream of internal improvements includes USAA's Image Processing System—technology that digitizes incoming mail for easy on-line viewing. Employees can retrieve any piece of customer mail in seconds. When customers call in reference to a letter they sent, employees say, "Yes, I have your letter right here in front of me." Customers would never believe they were talking to a $38 billion giant. USAA uses cutting-edge technology strategically to provide personal service cost-effectively. In fact, USAA's operating costs are the lowest in the industry—a full 12 percent lower than the industry average.

KNOW EXACTLY WHERE YOU'RE GOING

Rural/Metro Corporation captures as much information as possible from every point of contact with its customers. Like USAA, the emergency services company takes the next step—processing information with state-of-the-art technology to constantly improve the way it does business.

Rural/Metro formerly sent a firefighter to a customer's home for a fire safety inspection only when asked. Recognizing the fabulous opportunity to connect with customers, the company now offers a free inspection for every household once a year. Firefighters talk with the family and learn about any special needs or medical conditions. They also map out the home, noting the layout of rooms, the various entrances, and even where everybody sleeps.

Rural/Metro provides this service to be helpful to its customers, but has its own agenda as well—to build relationships and gather customer information to improve its level of service.

"Our computer aided dispatch service is linked to the 911 system," explains Fire Chief John Karolzak. "When a customer dials 911, our computer screen immediately displays all of that household's information—exactly how to get to the house, who's inside, where each person usually sleeps, and all of their special needs. If you have a son who's blind, it's on my screen when you call. If we show up on the scene and find you unconscious, we'll already know that you are diabetic, and be ready with the most appropriate treatment."

Additionally, Rural/Metro turns information readily available to all emergency services companies into a strategic advantage. "Most ambulance companies have ten ambulances going twenty-four hours a day," says John. "But most of the time, only four are needed—the other six are just parked, waiting for a call. For the past four years, we've tracked when and where calls happen by date, day of week, and time of day. We do a demand analysis and tailor our ambulance service accordingly. We know, for example, that on Sunday morning we don't need ten ambulances driving around. But on Friday night at one A.M., we definitely want all ten on the streets, constantly moving between the areas where calls are predicted to happen. We respond more quickly, get people to hospitals faster, and save lives and money because we predict emergencies, not just react to them."

Rural/Metro and USAA do more than collect customer feedback. They use their databases proactively to create personal relationships and better ways of doing business. What valuable information could you be using better?

INSIGHT TO ACTION

Insight 5: Make Technology Your Servant

Information Upgrade 5.0

❑ Like USAA, act on all customer feedback within twenty-four hours. Analyze trends later.

❑ What customer information do you need to enhance your services and products?

- Pull together what you already know.
- What's missing? Gather it.

❑ Leverage this information to develop new services and products.

❑ Use technology to put this important information in the hands of your people to provide more personal service.

Practice 17

Hit a Grand Slam

A technology grand slam is one seamlessly linked system that benefits your people, customers, and profits simultaneously. The resulting turbo boost propels your organization with a force that is greater than the sum of its parts.

- **Technology is good for people** when it works the way people do, increasing their capability and creativity. When systems are complicated and confusing, people spend half their time solving technical problems instead of serving customers. Develop human technology by involving customers and staff in its creation.
- **Technology is good for customers** when they have interactive, direct access to your company. Customer comments aren't simply acknowledged and forgotten—you capture feedback and take action.
- **Technology is good for profits** when it gives you much more in return than what you pay for it.

THE PLACE WHERE ALL THE MAGIC HAPPENS

Charles Schwab hit a grand slam when it created CustomBroker, an integrated information system that meets the diverse needs of its most profitable customers, active traders. Timely market information is an active trader's most treasured commodity. CustomBroker enables Schwab to deliver custom information the way each active trader wants it.

Schwab asks each active trader about the specific information he or she is interested in. A trader might respond, "Notify me if an earnings report becomes available on Sears stock, let me know how my AT&T stock is doing twice a day at ten A.M. and twelve noon, and get me any news reports that come up on the following fifteen companies . . ." Active trader phone representatives enter each customer's preferences into a computer. When an earnings report for Sears hits the wire, an "alert" chimes on the appropriate rep's computer, indicating which customer requested the update. The rep reviews the information and sends it off—via any medium the customer requests.

> *If you just throw technological tools into a culture that's not ready, people won't know how to use them, they won't want to use them, and they won't be motivated to learn how to use them.*
>
> —REGIS McKENNA,
> Chairman,
> Gemini-McKenna, Inc.

Reps can telephone, fax, send information via alphanumeric pager, or leave an e-mail message in a customer's StreetSmart software program. The computer tracks how each active trader prefers to receive information because it gets pretty confusing. "One customer wants phone calls before eleven A.M. when he's in his office," explains Bill Gerard, active trader phone rep. "On Tuesdays and Fridays, I send information to the pager in his golf cart, and I fax to his home the rest of the time." What information do your customers want to receive at a moment's notice?

Instant access to custom information makes all the difference for active traders. "I used to pay for the 'expertise' of the big brokers, thinking they knew more than I did," says Don Seta, a Schwab customer for nine years. "But as soon as I started using Schwab, something came alive in me I didn't know I had. I started analyzing information myself, making decisions on my own, and I've made a fortune in less than two years. A few years ago the S&P 500, the benchmark for the industry, was up 20 percent or so, which was a good year. My performance was about 84 percent. So now all I want is timely information—as much as I can get my hands on."

Active traders aren't the only ones delighted with CustomBroker. The technology is a boon for employees as well. "Since we got this stuff, my job is so much more fun," says Bill. "I have a better relationship with my customers. I don't have to put them on hold anymore while I walk across the room to flip through our book that was printed once a month. Everything is now on my desktop and updated daily. It's a much more intelligent conversation. The neat thing is customers usually have no idea what I have here on my desk. They just say, 'Hey, Bill's really on the ball today!'"

It's no accident Schwab developed an integrated system loved by employees and customers. Schwab programmers are "bizno-techies"—either experienced brokers who recently began programming or long-time programmers who sit in with Schwab brokers as they work. Bizno-techies understand both what technology can do *and* the realities of using it daily to serve customers.

Right in the middle of the Active Trader department is a door with a big sign that reads, "The Playpen." The room inside is jammed with computers of all shapes and sizes. Any bizno-techie with an idea runs to the Playpen to try it out immediately. "It's the fun place where all the magic happens," says Brent Threadgill of the Active Trader technology team.

The "magic" at Schwab is technology that's good for people, customers, and profits combined in one integrated information system.

TAKING CARE OF PATIENTS—NOT PAPERWORK

Harbor Hospital's transformation to patient-centered care required a major investment in technology. Needing systems that mirrored its new philosophy, the hospital installed technology to support its patients, staff, and bottom line—and experienced a turbo boost.

"In most hospitals, the nurse call system is anything but private," says Robin Orr. "You press a button from your bed and the loudspeaker throughout the wing booms, 'Mr. Jones, what would you like?' And then, just as loudly, 'I've got to go to the bathroom. Can somebody help me out of bed?' You just lie there and hope that someone comes to help."

Harbor redefines the patient experience. A new nurse-call system routes patient requests to a central communications center on the floor. When a call comes in, the patient's profile appears on-screen, complete with common requests and special information. Nurses and staff wear badges that transmit an infrared signal detected by sensors in every room and corridor. The person in the communications center knows exactly where everyone is and dispatches each patient request along with the room number to the appropriate staff member via alphanumeric pagers.

This technology allows Harbor to satisfy patients quickly, discreetly, and cost-effectively. "Maybe you want a glass of water, or maybe you're having a cardiac arrest," says Robin. "Those very different situations require a very different response. If it's cardiac arrest, we need the stat team to come with the paddles. But anyone can bring a glass of water."

At Harbor, technology liberates nurses to take care of patients. As nurses make their rounds, they enter each patient's temperature, blood pressure, and vital signs into a handheld computer the size of a TV remote control. The information is quickly uploaded at computer terminals located in recessed kiosks outside every sixth room. Every patient's medical records—vital signs, test results, and lab results—are on-line, accessible to all caregivers.

Where it used to take ninety minutes to get antibiotics, it now takes no time at all. A nurse simply walks to the automated medication dispenser cart located on each floor. She enters the patient's name and a screen displays which medication was prescribed and how many pills remain in the treatment. Then, just like an ATM, the machine dispenses the correct dosage.

"This type of technology allows caregivers to be in continuous touch with their patients," says Russell Coile, health care futurist. "They can spend more time at the patient's bedside rather than back in their bunkers filling out paperwork."

Barney Johnson, CEO, says Harbor's investment in technology is paying off. "My costs are about the same as those of other hospitals. Although not necessarily reducing the cost of healing, we are doing it better. It certainly increases the number of patients who want to be admitted. Word is getting out—it doesn't cost you any more to come to Harbor and you'll get a private room and personal care. It's definitely a market differentiator."

With a high-tech, high-touch approach to wellness, Harbor is reinventing the hospital of the future.

A $50 MILLION SAVINGS!

A typical major insurance company spends about $500 million a year on collision damages. ADP Claims Solutions Group partnered with its insurance customers to design technology that reduced the cost by 10 percent—a whopping $50 million savings!

ADP is the leader in providing claims processing, data communications, and information services to the insurance industry, but almost lost it all through complacency. The company had owned its market for twenty years, but let up on its development of new technologies. Competitors spotted the weakness and introduced superior products. ADP's strong customer relationships garnered a temporary reprieve, but customers made it clear: Regain technological leadership in one year or you're gone.

"By the time we realized our situation," says Gerhard Blendstrup, senior vice president of strategic service, "the very survival of our company was at stake. It was clear that incrementalism wouldn't work. We had to leapfrog the competition using technology in an innovative way."

ADP's number one priority was to improve the estimating procedure for automobile collision damages. Typically, when an auto accident occurs, the estimator analyzes the damage and cost of repair either with the customer or at a body shop. This process can take weeks and involves countless phone calls and piles of paperwork to verify the cost and availability of parts, not to mention labor costs.

The company spoke with its customers to find out

exactly what they needed. "You have to get out of your headset and into the headset of the customer," says Gerhard. "If you want technology to make people more productive, you must have the people who use it help design it—because you're not going to win unless your customer wants you to win."

ADP reestablished its leadership position with an easy-to-use technology that reduces the estimating process to minutes and requires absolutely no computer skills. The company created a comprehensive database containing millions of automobile parts, prices, availability, estimated repair times, and labor costs—all updated weekly and stored in a handheld computer. It has no keyboard, looks just like the old estimating tablet, and comes with a "magic" wand. When the estimator shows up, he touches the wand to the screen and selects the make, model, and year of the car. A picture of the car appears on the screen, and the estimator simply touches the wand to the damaged area. That area enlarges to show the fender, headlights, windshield, and so on. The estimator touches the parts needing replacement and up comes the cost of each part, including the total charge with labor.

ADP designed the technology to work the way human beings do. The technology itself is complex, but all the estimator needs is the handheld computer and magic wand. "You must use the computer to hide the computer," explains Gerhard. "Training times on the system for new estimators have been reduced to about three seconds—pick up the wand and touch the screen. And customers get more accurate estimates faster than ever."

ADP, Harbor Hospital, and Charles Schwab hit technology grand slams. They touch all the bases—people, customers, and profits. When you develop technology that's good for all three, your systems naturally support your people's skills, your customers' preferences, and the profitability of your business.

INSIGHT TO ACTION

Insight 5: Make Technology Your Servant

Hit a Grand Slam

❏ Create a technology wish list of three projects that will have the greatest impact on your people, customers, and profits.

- _____

- _____

- _____

❏ Evaluate where you'll get the biggest bang for your buck.

Technology Project	Estimated Cost	Projected ROI
_____	_____	_____
_____	_____	_____
_____	_____	_____

❏ Insist that frontline users and systems people work side by side from design to implementation. Involve customers every step of the way.

149

ENTHUSIASTIC
CUSTOMERS

INSPIRED
PEOPLE

FINANCIAL
PERFORMANCE

8. Lead with Care

7. Unleash the Power of People

6. Measure Well, Act Fast

5. Make Technology Your Servant

4. Simplify, Simplify, Simplify

3. Have the Courage to Set Bold Goals

2. Make Every Customer Feel Special

1. Build a Strong Foundation

Insight 6

Measure Well, Act Fast

In The Phantom Tollbooth, *after Milo learned about the power of perspectives at the Point of View, he traveled to Digitopolis, the city of numbers. There he met a curious fellow with twelve different faces called the Dodecahedron. The Dodecahedron was ecstatic to talk to his new acquaintance about numbers and measures—but he quickly noticed that Milo wasn't much interested in the subject:*

"Don't you know anything at all about numbers?"

"Well, I don't think they're very important," snapped Milo, too embarrassed to admit the truth.

"NOT IMPORTANT!" roared the Dodecahedron, turning red with fury. "Could you have tea for two without the two—or three blind mice without the three? Would there be four corners of the earth if there weren't a four? And how would *you sail the seven seas without a seven?"*

"All I meant was—" began Milo, but the
Dodecahedron, overcome with emotion and shout-
ing furiously, carried right on.

*"If you had high hopes, how would you know
how high they were? And did you know that nar-
row escapes come in all different widths? Would
you travel the whole wide world without ever
knowing how wide it was? And how could you do
anything at long last,"* he concluded, waving his
arms over his head, *"without knowing how long
the last was? Why numbers are the most beautiful
and valuable things in the world. Just follow me
and I will show you."*

As the Dodecahedron points out, numbers can be the
most valuable things in the world. Would you go on a diet
and not weigh yourself? Would you play a game if you
couldn't keep score? You can't reach your targets if you
don't know where you are, where you're going, and how
far you've come.

But like Milo, too many people ignore the value of numbers. Who can blame them? When you sit down at your
desk each morning to review another overwhelming bar-
rage of measurements, numbers quickly lose all meaning.
You're told measures are important, yet they never seem to
change anything. Companies spend millions on customer
research while the top customer issues remain unresolved.

KEEPING AN EYE ON THE SHOP

Measurement used to be instantaneous, meaningful, and gathered firsthand. A shopkeeper spent every day alongside his customers and products. He saw with his own eyes how people behaved and whether the shelves were empty or full. He knew right away which decisions were working and which were not. If the shopkeeper noticed that a customer of his had stopped coming into the store, he would go straight to the customer's house, knock on the door, and ask, "What's wrong?"

Today companies have locations around the world and process millions of customer transactions every day. Technology enables us to gather numbers on everything—and we do. Unfortunately, getting our arms around this mass of measurements is daunting, frustrating, and paralyzing.

Organizations can recapture the power of intimate, immediate feedback with innovative measurement systems, both simple and sophisticated. With its ECHO system, USAA spends every day alongside more than two million customers and doesn't miss a thing. Levi Strauss & Co.'s retail information system keeps the "company eye" on shelves around the world in order to replenish product immediately. Charles Schwab gathers customer feedback daily to hear right away what's working and what isn't. And when a frequent traveler stops coming to Marriott, the customer tracking system immediately generates a letter that asks "What's wrong?" and gives the customer an incentive to come back. These organizations learn what's most important to their customers, then use measurement systems to focus efforts on improving personal relationships and financial performance.

A good measurement system aligns your organization. It reveals where you're doing well, what calls for extra attention, and when a major course correction is needed. Good measures keep you focused on the customer, concentrate your efforts, and create a mandate for action.

An interviewer once asked Wayne Gretzky, the greatest hockey player of all time, "What's your secret?" Gretzky answered, "I just skate to where the puck is going to be." A good measurement system enables an entire organization to do this and more—to not only predict the future, but to reinvent it.

Practice 18   **THE WORLD ACCORDING TO TARP**

Practice 19   **MEASURE IN THE REAL WORLD**

Practice 20   **A FEW GOOD MEASURES**

Practice 21   **ENSURE WHAT GETS MEASURED GETS DONE**

Practice 18

The World According to TARP

Technical Assistance Research Programs, or TARP, is an international customer service research and consulting firm. It helps businesses develop complaint-handling and feedback systems to maximize customer enthusiasm and positive word of mouth. Many people are familiar with TARP's hallmark study on the cost of losing customers, but TARP also works with clients to tie customer measures to their bottom line and prioritize actions.

"There are four imperatives that must be addressed in order to establish an effective customer feedback system," says John Goodman, president of TARP. "With these fundamentals firmly in place, every measurement decision you make will be the right one."

1. DON'T CRIMINALIZE COMPLAINTS— SOLICIT THEM

Customers who complain reveal the issues most important to them *and* highlight where you need to improve. Handle a complaint well and the customer will be more loyal than if there was never a problem in the first place. But don't just fight fires—look hard at prevention. Keep in mind the complaints you actually hear are only the tip of the iceberg:

- *The customer complaints you hear about at headquarters or from your managers represent only 5 percent of unhappy customers. Only 50 percent complain at any level.*
- *More important, an average of 30 percent of those dissatisfied customers will not come back or buy again. WARNING: This number can be as high as 90 percent!*
- *These angry, departed customers tell their stories to up to ten other people, and 13 percent become "terrorists" who go out of their way to tell more than twenty people just to get even.*

2. PUT A PRICE TAG ON CUSTOMER DISSATISFACTION

"There must be an economic imperative associated with world-class quality and service," says John. "It's critical to have careful measurements that reveal the true dollar impact of customer satisfaction—and the lack of it." When you quantify the link between customer complaints and revenue, people stand up and take notice.

Consider a small chain of gas stations with 32,000 customers a year. Two hundred complain about leaky nozzles spilling gas on their cars. Management knows it would cost $4,000 to replace the nozzles, but since less than 1 percent of the customers complain, the expense doesn't seem worth it.

But remember, 200 complaints are just the tip of the iceberg—that's probably only 5 percent of the dissatisfied customers. In actuality, 4,000 customers are unhappy pumping gas with a leaky nozzle. TARP research shows that, on average, 30 percent of all dissatisfied customers will not come back—that's 1,200 lost customers. If each customer spends $750 a year on gas, the company has just lost $900,000 a year. Furthermore, TARP shows that each of these 1,200 departed customers tells an average of five friends about the experience, increasing the loss to the company. Replacing the leaky nozzles is now clearly seen as a $4,000 insurance policy against a minimum $900,000 loss. Identify the "leaky nozzles" in your company—how much are they costing you?

3. PINPOINT THE NATURE OF THE PROBLEM

Complaints reveal which issues are most important to your customers, but that's not good enough. There's usually one specific problem fueling a customer's displeasure. Find out exactly what bugs your customers the most—the key point of pain—and fix it. Focusing your resources saves time and money and provides a huge return on investment.

A major U.S. transportation company consulted TARP to identify the root cause of its customers' dissatisfaction. The company's revenues were dropping along with its customer satisfaction scores. Customers complained most often about cleanliness and delayed trains. These were difficult problems. With thousands of cars and stations, "cleanliness" was an ambiguous and expensive issue for the company to tackle. The "on-time" problem involved its entire infrastructure of computers, cars, and rails—to upgrade everything would cost billions.

TARP undertook a comprehensive survey of passengers. Customers cited bathrooms as the major cleanliness problem area, but TARP found that bathroom odor was specifically mentioned most of the time. Additionally, TARP discovered that customers weren't frustrated with delays per se, they were angry about not knowing the nature of the problem or how long the delay would be.

TARP pinpointed two problem areas that the company could fix cost-effectively to satisfy the majority of unhappy customers. The company improved the odor in the bathrooms and intensified its efforts to keep them clean. The company also installed a new communication system enabling conductors to keep passengers updated when delays occurred. Now, as soon as the train comes to a stop, passengers hear, "This is your conductor. We'll be stopped for about five minutes to check out something on the tracks. If it's longer than that, we'll let you know."

Rather than investing billions of dollars in overall cleanliness and infrastructure, the company could spend less than $20 million on two of its most significant problems and transform most of its unhappy customers into happy ones.

4. MEASURE YOUR PROGRESS CONSTANTLY

Most companies believe that when it comes to measuring customer enthusiasm, a yearly "Do you love us?" survey is sufficient. Meanwhile, financial data is scrutinized daily. Losing customers directly impacts your bottom line. Identify the key drivers of customer enthusiasm and measure them at least once a month. Report the results as rigorously as the financials—then act quickly to make improvements.

These four pillars support every good measurement system. Master these fundamentals, and you'll be ready to listen to your customers, keep your measurements focused, and translate feedback into commitment and action.

INSIGHT TO ACTION
Insight 6: Measure Well, Act Fast

The World According to TARP

How much is a problem costing you?
Is it worth fixing?

❑ Determine the annual worth of a customer:

_____ × $_____ = $ _____

| Transactions per year | $ profit per transaction | Worth of customer |

❑ Calculate the yearly cost of the problem (keep in mind that this figure does not include the cost of negative word of mouth!):

_____ × 20 × .30 × $_____ = $_____

| Number of complaints | Only 5% tell you | 30% won't return | Worth of customer | Cost of problem per year |

❑ Determine your return on investment (ROI) when you fix the problem:

$ _____ ÷ $ _____ = $ _____

| Cost of problem per year | Cost of fixing problem | (ROI) |

❑ Based on ROI for various problems, invest in solving problems with the greatest payback.

Practice 19

Measure in the Real World

Many years ago, the American Textile Manufacturers Institute wanted to learn which colors of fabric women liked most. If manufacturers could produce these colors in bulk, they would lower their costs substantially. The institute had Louis Cheskin, the premier researcher of his time, undertake this massive project.

Cheskin rented out Madison Square Garden for one week. He ran ads in all the New York papers offering women ten dollars to come down and give their opinions. Women flocked to take advantage of the offer. They arrived to find a hundred tables, each piled high with beautiful scarves of a particular color. Each woman was asked to walk among the tables and rate each color from one to ten on a scorecard. After turning in her scorecard and collecting her ten dollars, each woman was allowed to take home the scarf of her choice as a special thank-you.

By the end of the week there were thousands of score-cards to tally. Someone from the Textile Manufacturers Institute, anxious for the results, asked, "When can we start tabulating?"

"We're not going to look at the scorecards," Cheskin replied. "We're going to throw them all away. Each table was stocked with the same number of scarves. We'll simply count the scarves that remain. Who cares how the colors were rated on a scorecard—we're interested in the colors women actually chose."

Products and services should be designed around what the customer wants. But all too often management makes decisions based on what it *thinks* customers want. Or it asks customers to react to hypothetical situations and surveys, typically with misleading results.

As the story of the scarves demonstrates, you can measure reality by polling customers in situations that emulate real-world transactions. Miller SQA and Marriott discovered that measuring what customers want and how they behave in the real world takes a little creativity, but really pays off.

CAUGHT IN A VICIOUS CYCLE OF IMPROVEMENT

Miller SQA, a subsidiary of Herman Miller, used to ask customers the same old questions: What did we do well?

What did we do poorly? What can we improve? Not surprisingly, these questions rarely prompted passionate, useful feedback. Miller SQA finally realized that if the aim is enthusiastic customers, why not ask them about the last time they were dazzled? Now the company asks customers just one question: "What was your most wonderful experience with Miller SQA?"

Gary VanSpronsen says measuring enthusiasm created enthusiasm. With the feedback generated from this simple question, Miller SQA pointed the company in a new direction. In the last four years Miller SQA has quadrupled its business, enjoying 35 percent compounded growth in sales and profits.

"It may be that we provided world-class service for only ten seconds," Gary points out, "but from our customers' stories, we understand exactly what occurred during those ten seconds that made such a lasting impression and blew their minds. We get real clarity about what is important to them."

Armed with such powerful and emotional responses, Miller SQA recognized three key aspects that drive its customers' enthusiasm:

- **Reliability:** Do what you say you're going to do.
- **Responsiveness:** Be available and quick.
- **Empathy:** Relate to the customer as a person, not an order.

And Miller SQA doesn't stop there. From customer stories, the company learns exactly which systems, cultural aspects, and leadership practices made the "ten seconds of world-class service" possible. Or as Gary puts it, "We *stalk*, *fan*, and *amplify* the elements of excellence. First, we get as close as possible to what's important to our customers through their stories. Then we set the lessons ablaze and fan them until they're huge and obvious to everyone. Finally, we replicate those same capabilities throughout the company."

Thanks to its creative questioning, Miller SQA ends up with hundreds of fantastic stories to share with its people and potential customers. "The recognition cranks up our performance even more," says Gary. "If you're not careful, you're soon caught in a vicious cycle of improvement."

THE PEOPLE'S COURTYARD

Courtyard by Marriott, the company's moderately priced hotel chain, runs an annual occupancy 13 percent higher than the industry average. It is growing rapidly, with 500 properties planned by the year 2000. Courtyard's success is the direct result of real-world customer measures.

When Marriott decided to enter the mid-price lodging market, it could have simply created a smaller, less expensive version of its highly successful upscale hotel chain. "But we wanted to do something different," explains brand vice president Craig Lambert, who was part of the Courtyard by Marriott design team. "We wanted to break some old paradigms, so the ideas couldn't come from us.

We had to get very clear on the customers' needs. Since we wanted to deliver high-quality service at a low price, we knew we'd have to give up some things. But that was for our customers to decide—they must always drive the decision process."

Marriott put the design of the new hotel into the hands of its customers—literally. The company leased a large warehouse and built adjustable prototype rooms inside. It invited business travelers, families, and other potential customers to help design the rooms. Customers could arrange the TV, the bed, and the desk, for example. Marriott could move the walls to understand what size of room felt too small, what felt cozy, and what was deluxe.

The company wanted to know which amenities were indispensable and which could be left out. But when the design team gave customers a checklist of items and asked which they wanted in their hotel room, the response was, "All of them!"

> Never prophesize—especially about the future.
>
> —MARK TWAIN

Marriott came up with a way to get beyond what customers wished for and determine what they were willing to *pay* for. Researchers gave each participant a fictional forty-nine dollars with which to "build" his or her hotel room. Customers had sixty cards, each listing a single amenity and its estimated cost to Marriott. An additional phone, for example, was two dollars, a VCR was four dollars, and a bigger bathroom nine dollars. Customers perused the cards and selected what they wanted. If they went over the forty-nine-dollar budget, they had to either eliminate features or choose less expensive ones. Customers were forced to make realistic trade-offs.

Courtyard is a success precisely because Marriott emulated real-world transactions to measure what customers wanted. But people's needs and priorities change quickly, so Courtyard looks at customer feedback monthly to stay on track. For example, the original design included video arcade games, since replaced by StairMasters and LifeCycles. Every five years Courtyard goes through its intense, customer-driven design process all over again to ensure it remains "the hotel designed by business travelers."

Marriott used the Courtyard design process for its Fairfield Inn chain, and currently has three other projects in the works that are being conceived and built the same way—with the customer in control.

Craig Lambert knows the power of measuring in the real world. "Marriott now lets the customer drive design. We have an ongoing process to make sure we are focused on what our customers want and not what we *think* our customers want. There's a big, big difference."

Marriot designed a new hotel chain from scratch using real-world customer measures. Miller SQA quadrupled its business in four years. What can such measures do for you?

INSIGHT TO ACTION

Insight 6: Measure Well, Act Fast

Measure in the Real World

❑ Have each manager ask three customers monthly: What was your most wonderful experience with us? What was your worst experience with us?

❑ Gather and share the good experiences with your people and existing/potential customers. Find ways to replicate them.

❑ Gather the worst experiences and prioritize and fix the most common problems.

❑ Have your customers play an active role in designing your new products and services.

Practice 20
A Few Good Measures

You can't measure everything. There are only so many reports, figures, and printouts the human mind can handle. Who hasn't been numbed by numbers and dazed by data? The fact is that the more you measure, the more diluted your efforts become. Measures guide an organization, so a random, frenetic, and unfocused measurement system is sure to lead a company in a similar direction.

A few pertinent measures, on the other hand, can be looked at, managed, and *understood*. Developing a small number of vital measures ensures that you have an eye on the essentials. The goal is to build a balanced, integrated organization with turned-on people, enthusiastic customers, *and* strong profits. Challenge yourself to look at people, customers, and profits in equal measure.

RESTORING FOCUS

While many American textile companies have closed their doors, Milliken & Company, winner of the Malcolm-

Baldrige National Quality Award, thrives. President Tom Malone used to sit down every week and pore over the 100-plus measures his company was "focusing" on. He reflected on the words of his friend Bob Galvin, chairman of Motorola: "Anything can and should be measured if you want to improve it." But with so many numbers to stay on top of, Tom found himself thinking, "Is it possible to be measuring *too much stuff*? Our associates need to measure those things they want to improve, but I can't effectively review this many measures!"

Milliken sorely needed a few good measures—something focused, meaningful, and manageable. The company now uses a unique measurement system that restores integration and balance on both a corporate and departmental level.

Each year Tom Malone and his executive team get together to review associate satisfaction, customer feedback, and financial results. They then target two or three major priorities to measure and drive for the year (in 1996, for example, the vital areas were customer satisfaction, cost reduction, and profitable growth). Tom and his team are now truly focused.

Senior management works with each business and support area to develop its own set of concrete measures that support the corporate priorities. "If you try to give the same measures to everybody in an organization, it isn't going to work," Tom points out. "If the measures don't fit a division, it'll say, 'Why in the heck are you making me do all these crazy measures that aren't important to our area?' If we're trying to grow a new division, we don't want it obsessed with cutting costs—but another more mature division can do a lot to reduce costs. So the people in each area decide on two or three measurements that are relevant for them. When all is said and done, each department's measures add up to the company reaching its very focused objectives."

Milliken's multitiered, integrated system allows each department to develop its own set of vital measures, yet ensures that the company as a whole is measuring and driving a small number of appropriate priorities. "Measures must be meaningful again on a very personal level," says Tom. "That's the only way they can work. If you're not keeping score, you're just practicing!"

BALANCING MISSION AND MARGIN

Milliken learned to limit its number of measures, but many organizations have another problem—they don't balance people, customer, and profit measures. Measuring financial performance is critical, but the key to long-term vitality is a balanced scorecard.

Like every organization, Harbor Hospital must keep costs as low as possible. But having implemented patient-centered care, the hospital now seeks to cut costs and complexity while simultaneously *increasing* the level of personal care provided to patients and the community. Harbor's measurement system had to follow suit.

Because Harbor cares deeply about each patient's experience it solicits feedback via surveys, focus groups, and follow-up calls. The hospital even tracks letters written to caregivers. It found that patient satisfaction is directly linked to the quality and timeliness of medical care, the caring attitude of the staff, and the accessibility of information.

Measuring what's important to patients resulted in vast improvements in those areas. In the last year admitting time was cut in half, the time to initiate a physician's order for critical medication and tests was reduced by 50 percent, and the wait to receive antibiotics went down 74 percent. Consequently, patient satisfaction rose to 98 percent. Most important, patients say they feel cared for in a way that respects them as individuals.

Caregiver satisfaction is carefully monitored as well through surveys, staff meetings, and turnover rates. Interestingly, when the first patient-centered floor opened, turnover increased—staff who didn't want to be accountable for reducing the cost and complexity of care left. The remaining staff are happier and more committed than ever. Nurses love the open communication, spirit of teamwork, and continuity of care.

Harbor still tracks the financials—occupancy rates, patient lengths of stay, readmittance rates, and nonessential return visits—but one financial measure is now paramount: *how* money is spent. "Typically," says Robin Orr, "for every dollar a hospital spends on direct care, four dollars are spent waiting for care to happen, arranging for it, and writing it down."

Harbor is still a work in progress but works hard to balance its mission and margins by integrating people, patient, and financial measures. Milliken took a frenetic and unfocused system and distilled from it three vital measurements. Both discovered the centering power of a few good measures.

INSIGHT TO ACTION

Insight 6: Measure Well, Act Fast

A Few Good Measures

❑ List your company's top three strategic priorities and measures. Make sure they are in sync.

Priorities	Measures
_____	_____
_____	_____
_____	_____

❑ Have each individual and department do the same, and make sure they are in sync.

Company Priorities	Department/ Individual Priorities	Department/ Individual Measures
_____	_____	_____
_____	_____	_____
_____	_____	_____

Practice 21

Ensure What Gets Measured Gets Done

There is a homely adage which runs, "Speak softly and carry a big stick; you will go far."

—THEODORE ROOSEVELT

Your measures may be accurate and real-world. They may be balanced and integrated. But if you don't translate measures into action, you may as well throw them out the window. You probably have more than your fair share of customer surveys, market research reports, and morale surveys. But is this information presented and discussed, then quickly forgotten?

Chances are that simply asking your people to take action won't do the trick. Ensure what gets measured gets done. Hold people accountable for turning measures into action.

- Tie performance to financial incentives.
- Involve senior management.
- Cultivate an action-oriented culture.

TURNING EXPECTATIONS INTO REALITY

Intel's corporate customer satisfaction scores have reached peaks of 40 percent improvement in the last three years—largely due to an action-oriented measurement system designed to make Intel the vendor of choice in its industry. Every quarter the company dispatches representatives to its most important corporate customers. Reps ask customers to rate the importance of eight key areas from one to ten. Then, using the same scale, customers judge Intel's performance in those areas. If there's a discrepancy, reps ask what Intel can do to improve and if other vendors are performing better.

When the discrepancy between importance and performance ratings is three or greater, the department responsible is notified immediately. Specific actions to close the gap are written into the department business plan for the next quarter—ensuring that Intel remains vendor of choice.

Intel goes even further with its Executive Sponsor Program. A senior executive is assigned to each of the corporate customers polled. The executive owns the relationship at the top level. "The vendor of choice survey opens a dialogue and enhances personal relationships," explains

Peter Glass of Intel quality strategic programs. "But we've learned that as the relationships with customers grow and deepen, so does the quality of the feedback they give us. Our progress as a company ultimately depends on relationships, and we put those relationships in the hands of our senior people."

Intel measures the gap between its customers' expectations and reality and turns those measures into action. Holding both departments and senior executives responsible for closing that gap ensures that what Intel measures gets done.

MOBILIZING PEOPLE TO DELIVER

Datatec Industries provides local- and wide-area network design, installation, and support services for large *Fortune* 500 companies throughout the United States and Europe. Like Intel, the company measures what its customers want and takes action to deliver. Datatec's inspired workforce dazzles its customers, demonstrated by revenue growth of 180 percent in just five years. But CEO Chris Carey remembers when things weren't so rosy. "Our quality of service was so bad, customers were constantly calling to complain. Our front office people were continually handling complaints to the point where they didn't want to answer the phones."

When Datatec lost its largest client, McDonald's, Chris realized that a shift in culture, priorities, and measures was imperative. "Back then, we only asked customers about things that were important to *us*. We're a technology company, so naturally we wanted to know if our systems were functioning properly—and they were. So we thought, 'What's the problem?' But once we began talking to customers to understand what *they* cared about, everyone in our organization learned exactly what to concentrate on. Our measures took on a whole new look."

Today, a member of the quality department contacts the customer's site manager twenty-four hours after a job is complete. He measures what Datatec's customers care about: overall quality, timeliness, quality of communications, cleanliness of the job site, and whether or not the customer received a thank-you card complete with the home phone numbers of Datatec's senior executives.

> Inactivity is the darkroom where negatives develop.
>
> —KATHY HELOU,
> National Sales
> Director,
> Mary Kay Cosmetics

Measuring what's important to the *customer* was a strategic breakthrough, but Datatec takes the next step—mobilizing its people to *deliver*. Site manager surveys are tallied and translated into a performance rating for every employee. Those few who don't satisfy 100 percent of their customers are coached to improve their performance. Annual bonuses are paid out according to overall customer satisfaction scores. "This company really started moving and changing when we tied customer measures back to individuals and their bonuses," Chris explains.

Datatec's measurement system engages senior management as well. Like Intel, Datatec assigns a senior executive to each of its customers. At least once a year, they sit down and talk about how to better meet each other's needs. The partnership is strengthened with questions such as . . .

How would you rate the overall quality of Datatec's

- communication with you?
- responsiveness to your needs?
- understanding of your business?
- support of your business objectives?

Chris says this level of involvement makes a huge difference. "Getting executives involved with customer satisfaction measures teaches them to lead and make decisions based on more than just the P&L."

Datatec translates measures into action, creating a customer-obsessed company in the process. Customer satisfaction tops 97 percent, and employee turnover has dropped a full 50 percent in three years. The phones still ring off the hook, but employees happily answer them. They know these calls are from turned on customers, not frustrated ones.

WALL-TO-WALL ACTION

Peter McIntosh of Charles Schwab also transforms measures into action. In contrast to Intel and Datatec, he doesn't use financial incentives or executive involvement. Peter simply creates a culture in which taking action is paramount. "I have measures up on the wall for all to see. I say, 'Keep looking at them. Understand this is what I want to do. If you're working on something else, you better reconsider.' I want transfers faster. I want dividends paid faster. I want things cleaned up—reconciled daily rather than monthly. That's what I want. Everyone better be working toward those goals."

Peter sets inspirational targets and liberates his people to get the job done. "I don't know what a good reject rate is. We just write them all down and put them up on the wall where everyone can see. We wrote 22 percent at first. And all of a sudden, the number just plummeted. It's now less than 10 percent—and getting lower." His people are so motivated that when they see a measure, they naturally want to improve it. This is no small feat. Simply tacking measures to the wall does not inspire people to action. It takes a culture of optimism and commitment to fuel such excitement and ingenuity.

Stressing the importance of measures is one thing. Doing something about them is another. Inspire your people to action. Get incentives, management, and culture on your side.

INSIGHT TO ACTION

Insight 6: Measure Well, Act Fast

Ensure What Gets Measured Gets Done

❑ Have top customers rank what's most important to them, and your performance on each.

Most Important	Ranking (1–10)	Performance (1–10)	Gap
_____	_____	_____	_____
_____	_____	_____	_____
_____	_____	_____	_____

❑ Take action to improve areas with the biggest gaps between importance and performance.

❑ Post a visual scorecard to track monthly progress. Discuss the results constantly.

❑ Make senior executives responsible for relationships with top customers.

ENTHUSIASTIC CUSTOMERS

INSPIRED PEOPLE

FINANCIAL PERFORMANCE

8. Lead with Care

7. Unleash the Power of People

6. Measure Well, Act Fast

5. Make Technology Your Servant

4. Simplify, Simplify, Simplify

3. Have the Courage to Set Bold Goals

2. Make Every Customer Feel Special

1. Build a Strong Foundation

Insight 7

Unleash the Power of People

I watched Tommy, a friend of my son, Blake, strike out for about the fiftieth time that year. He must have hit the strikeout threshold, because he threw his bat in the dirt and went back to the bench, sobbing uncontrollably. Blake was the next batter. He struck out, too, ending the game. The team had lost, as it had every Little League game that year.

Blake was quiet as we drove home. "It's just a game," I offered.

"Dad, I can't hit the ball," Blake burst out. "Do you know Tommy and me are the only guys on the team without a hit all year? At school, the other kids call us 'The Strikeout Kings.'"

"Tell you what," I said. "This week, before your last game, we're going to practice one thing: how to hit the ball."

I taught him everything my father and coaches had taught me—have a nice level swing, watch the ball meet the bat, and don't try to kill it.

In the final game of the season, Tommy got up to bat and smacked a double on the very first pitch. Tommy was on second base, a place he'd never been in his life, beaming from ear to ear. I looked over to remind Blake about what we'd worked on, but he was already striding toward the batter's box.

He barely missed the first two pitches. "This is going to be awful," I thought. But on the next pitch, Blake stuck out his bat and hit a home run. A Little League home run, that is, with a throw here, a throw there, a throw everywhere—but a home run all the same. As the two boys headed for home, the entire team came flying off the bench. The team's confidence soared and it went on to win for the first and only time that season.

Driving home I exclaimed, "I'm so proud of you! A home run on your first hit! It just goes to show the value of good coaching."

Blake looked at me like I was crazy. "That had nothing to do with it, Dad. When I saw Tommy hit the ball, I said to myself, 'If Tommy can do it, so can I.'"

Blake didn't want to be an outcast at school; he wanted to belong. He didn't want to be the only player on the team who hadn't made a contribution; he knew he was better than that. And when he saw Tommy finally get a hit, he knew he could, too.

The need to belong, improve, and make a meaningful contribution is not unique to little boys playing baseball. We all want to achieve our potential and be an important part of the team.

Just as Blake succeeded after observing his peer in action, real learning happens in the workplace, not in the classroom. Often the best coaches are the other players. Who are your best people? Let them develop your team. "Listen to me—I've been in this business for twenty years . . ." has far less impact than, "This is Susan, probably one of our best people in sales. You're going to work side by side with her. She'll teach you more in two weeks than I could in two years."

Today bureaucracy, reengineering, and downsizing rob organizations of trust and a sense of community. But it doesn't have to be that way. People give everything they've got when they are valued members of a meaningful team. Create an environment of teamwork, support, and learning. Encourage people to greatness. The desire to excel comes from inside.

Provide your people with an abundance of those two commodities in shortest supply and greatest demand in our society: a sense of purpose and a feeling of community. A bit of freedom, a bit of human connection, and a chance to contribute to a worthy cause awakens the home-run hitter in all of us.

Practice 22

Hire the Head and the Heart

A farmer in need of a farmhand posted a notice in the village. Three promising youths responded, and the farmer met with each in turn. He asked the first young man about his background, and concluded with a peculiar question. "Tell me, how long can you work with a stone in your shoe?"

"Half a day," answered the youth. The farmer thanked him and sent him on his way.

The farmer spoke with the second young man, again concluding with "How long can you work with a stone in your shoe?"

"All day long!" boasted the boy. The farmer sent the second young man on his way.

The farmer met with the third youth. "How long can you work with a stone in your shoe?"

*"Not a minute!" exclaimed the youth. "When I get a
stone in my shoe, I take it out right away."*
The farmer hired the third young man on the spot.

The farmer in this American folktale wanted someone
with not only the right skills, but heart—the desire, initiative, and independence to solve problems immediately.
The farmer formulated the right question to find the right
person.

- **Hire the heart**. You can teach skills, but you can't
  teach passion and personality. Find provocateurs with
  the character to take you to a new level.
- **Hire people who will naturally succeed.** Don't wait
  until the ninety-day probation is over before deciding
  if you've got the right person for the job. Profile your
  top performers, learn what makes them tick, and hire
  people just like them. For the best possible fit, let your
  people interview and hire who they want on their
  team.

EVERYONE HAS A GIFT—HIRE A NATURAL

The Ritz-Carlton consistently outperforms its competitors
because the individuals at Ritz-Carlton are top performers
themselves. This is no accident. The Ritz-Carlton developed a hiring process to secure the best person for any
particular postion. The company's philosophy is that

everyone has certain unique talents. These talents are not learned—they are gifts that allow people to excel naturally and spontaneously in a particular area.

The Ritz-Carlton surveys its best performers to understand what makes them different from the average employee. The company analyzes the responses and compiles a set of interview questions for each position in the hotel. The questions identify those applicants with the greatest potential for success.

Prospective salespeople who answer questions like top performers do, for example, turn out to be top performers themselves. They generally sell twice as much as people who don't match the profile. Ritz-Carlton discovered that there exists a natural salesperson, a natural housekeeper, a natural front-desk agent, and a natural bellperson. Its goal is to fill every position in every hotel with just such a natural. "We can only teach so much technique," explains Larry Sternberg, director of human resources for The Ritz-Carlton Singapore. "The rest is what you have in your heart."

The Ritz-Carlton ensures a great fit by putting the hiring process directly into the hands of the workers. A front-desk agent, for example, interviews applicants and introduces the top candidates to the rest of the front-desk team. The team decides if an applicant's skills and personality complement the group.

The Ritz-Carlton formulates the right questions to get the "naturals" it wants and lets its people choose who they work with. The result is talented people who excel at the right job and have fun doing it—and the lowest turnover rate in the industry. Find out what makes your best people tick and identify the naturals for your business.

THE HEART OF THE MATTER

Why are so many organizations blind to anything but previous experience, education, and first impressions when deciding who to hire? It doesn't matter where people come from. What matters is that they have the heart for the job.

Andy Sorenson, general manager of the Courtyard by Marriott Hotel in Norwood, Massachusetts, needed additional housekeeping staff. Area unemployment was low and the Marriott culture strongly encourages good citizenship, so Andy looked into the possibility of bringing in people with disabilities to clean rooms. Out of a business need, Andy discovered a whole new way of working.

Andy contacted a local assistance group that helped him identify ten individuals with disabilities to work in housekeeping. The initial training took more time and other hotel associates were skeptical at first. But Andy says the new workers quickly became an important part of the team.

"It's so much fun to work with them. Michelle is the biggest Boston Bruins fan and we always go over the play-by-play the day after a game. At the company picnic, we couldn't get Phil off the karaoke stage because he was having so much fun. We can't imagine life without them. We all get along really well. They bring us life and happiness every single day. They're dependable, have a great attitude, and are thankful for what they've got. We all see ourselves in a different light."

Andy and his crew learned to ignore the labels placed on people. Instead of seeing the word "disability" and focusing on all the things people can't do, why not look at all the things people can do? "There are things that I can't do," says Andy. "I can't dunk a basketball. Does that make me a bad guy? No, it means I can't play for the New York Knicks, but I can do other things. People with disabili-ties do the same things we do, just in a different way. They may open a jar a little differently because they only have two fingers, or they may need special devices to get around. If it requires me to alter the way we do work a bit, it's not a problem. The benefits they bring far outweigh any little changes I have to make."

> *Most of the time professionals think only with their intellect. It's time to start thinking with the heart.*
>
> —BEVERLEY WILSON, Advanced Trainer of Trainers, Health Realization Model

Customers have been incredibly supportive. "Occasionally, a guest comes to my office to see me," says Andy. "I prepare myself to handle a complaint, but most of the time they say, 'I just wanted to tell you that I think what you're doing is absolutely fantastic! I will always stay at your hotel.' That's pretty rewarding."

Andy took a risk and hired the heart. He found people

who get the work done *and* whose mere presence takes his people and hotel to a new level. The Ritz-Carlton looks for something special inside—natural talent that complements the position. The benefits that a passionate soul brings to your business are worth their weight in degrees and credentials.

INSIGHT TO ACTION

Insight 7: Unleash the Power of People

Hire the Head and the Heart

❑ Validate success criteria for all jobs based on your best performers and company values.

❑ Use these criteria to be sure applicants

- mirror top performers.
- are provocateurs with passion, conviction, and creativity.

❑ Let your best people do the hiring for their team.

❑ With Andy Sorenson's experience in mind, come up with two nontraditional sources for new people.

- _____
- _____

Practice 23

Sow the Seeds of Greatness

"Kathy Helou! Come on down!" cried the announcer's voice. "You're the next contestant on The Price Is Right!*" A twenty-seven-year-old girl with bright blue eye shadow and a halter top came screeching down the aisle. After accidentally guessing the correct price of a computer, Kathy was up on stage with host Bob Barker. "What do we have for Kathy today?" Bob asked. A red curtain swished open as the voice boomed, "A brand-new CAAAAAR!"*

If Kathy could match four prices with the correct items that new car would be all hers. But Kathy only got one price right, and that was the prize she won— an assortment of Mary Kay products.

Kathy Helou appeared on the TV game show during medical leave from her job as an executive secretary at a

Fortune 500 company. She was diagnosed with anorexia nervosa and ordered to take some time off. Her husband took her to California, where they visited a few game shows as a form of therapy.

The prize Kathy won also included a complimentary facial by a local Mary Kay consultant. Kathy loved the products, and the consultant, along with her husband and friends, suggested she sell Mary Kay cosmetics herself. Her self-esteem was very low—being on display as a spokeswoman for beauty was a terrifying prospect. But the women Kathy met through Mary Kay—people of strength and power leading meaningful lives and making their own choices—were incredibly inspirational. Although foreign to Kathy, something inside told her that she wanted that, too.

> There's a little genius in all of us. We're all closet geniuses.
>
> —JERRY WILLIAMS,
> Oakland, California,
> Community Police
> Officer

Today Kathy is the paragon of health, vitality, and inspiration, and she thanks the nurturing environment of Mary Kay. Last year, as a national sales director, she earned over $400,000.

BACK TO NURTURE

Mary Kay Cosmetics nurtures Kathy and 450,000 other women from all walks of life. One national sales director used to work the graveyard shift packing shotgun shells.

Another was a law student. Accountants, managers, bankers, doctors, homemakers, and teachers are leaving their jobs and flocking to Mary Kay—because Mary Kay sows the seeds of greatness.

Mary Kay builds an environment of trust, respect, and support, then gives people everything they need to succeed—opportunities to learn and profit in an exciting work atmosphere.

CREATE AN ENVIRONMENT OF TRUST AND RESPECT

Advancement at Mary Kay depends partly on the success of a beauty consultant's recruits, so friendship and mentoring become more important than competition. Mary Kay values and respects people for their uniqueness, letting everyone succeed in their own way. "Mary Kay recognizes people for who they are, teaches them the basic skills of the job, and then just lets people rise when they are ready," says Kathy. "It's so much fun for me as a director to watch people go through their own metamorphosis. They are caught in their cocoon at first, and then they start to achieve little breakthroughs. I love watching them emerge as beautiful butterflies. And everybody gets to help them out by nurturing and fostering them through praise and encouragement."

PROVIDE OPPORTUNITIES FOR PERSONAL AND FINANCIAL GROWTH

Mary Kay provides beauty consultants with the support and resources they need to grow, learn, and contribute. Seminars, videos, books, audiotapes, and mentors help them achieve their personal best in business and life. "The room for personal improvement is the biggest room in anybody's house," says Arlene Lenarz, national sales director. "Mary Kay is a self-improvement course we get paid for taking."

Financial opportunities are unlimited. The number of national sales director and director positions is not fixed—anyone who meets the sales and recruiting requirements becomes one. Mary Kay turns more women into millionaires than any other company in the world. Hundreds of women earn six-figure annual incomes.

> *Our competitive advantage is sharing opportunities with others.*
>
> —LARRY HARLEY, President, Mary Kay Cosmetics, U.S.

MAKE WORK FUN AND EXCITING

Fun and excitement are the secret ingredients at Mary Kay, creating a sense of enthusiasm and camaraderie that is unstoppable. Weekly sales meetings are held worldwide to cheer each other on and share "I Stories"—personal success stories like Kathy Helou's. But Seminar, Mary Kay's $6 million celebration, tops everything.

"I have been at this company for eleven years," says Rhonda Shasteen, director of sales and leadership training. "I've organized and attended forty-four Seminars. But on every opening day, when Mary Kay Ash walks onto that stage with 50,000 screaming women and the organ blasting the 'Mary Kay Enthusiasm Song,' I lose it. I just bawl and squeal. You feel the energy in that room and it sends chills up your spine. It's bigger than the Academy Awards. Seminar is a life-altering experience."

At Seminar beauty consultants attend classes and lectures, test new products, network, and get charged up for the coming year. Beauty consultants pay a fee and their own travel expenses as an investment in their own learning. Yet women hover over the mailbox, check in hand, waiting for the registration form. Can you imagine your people fighting to get into one of your corporate training sessions?

SPEED IS THE MAGIC INGREDIENT

Mary Kay beauty consultants thrive in an atmosphere of trust, growth, and excitement. But every corporate culture is different. Create an environment where *your* people can be great.

Peter McIntosh of Schwab discovered that his people

want to move quickly. "Speed is the magic ingredient," he says. "People work best when they can go fast. Speed turns an organization on. It energizes and incites people, it makes them want to get involved. People who know what they're doing like to go fast. And even more important, people that *don't* know what they're doing *don't* like to go fast. So I announce we're going to go fast and guess what happens? Some say, 'Gee, I'm not sure I want to play.' That's great, don't. Others say, 'I kind of like it!' Speed attracts the right kind of people and repels the wrong kind."

People want to be trusted and respected. They want to move fast in an inspiring, creative setting. When you create an environment where people can be great, they will turn on your customers and profits.

INSIGHT TO ACTION

Insight 7: Unleash the Power of People

Sow the Seeds of Greatness

❑ Brainstorm with your team: "What would make this a great place to work?" Take steps to make it a reality.

❑ Start off every meeting with one or two people sharing personal success stories. Discuss lessons learned and how to apply them.

❑ Find ways to make people feel special and valued every day.

❑ Once you know where you want to go, increase the velocity—get there fast.

Practice 24

Build a Winning Team

The best professional golfers usually win tournament rounds with a score of four or five under par. But in a "scramble" tournament, four average golfers (like us) always outscore the pros. Each player tees off and the foursome decides whose ball is in the best position for the next shot. Each player on the team then moves his or her ball to that spot, hits again, and the process repeats—bringing in scores of six to eight strokes under par. If a team of average golfers, using everyone's best shots, can do better than the pros, just imagine what they could do working together in a business they know well.

Does your team thrive on each person's best contribution? When people work well together, the synergy they create takes them much further than they can go as individuals. Three things are crucial to keep a winning team on track:

- **Keep the team focused on the big picture.** People are more committed when they understand their role in achieving the overall goal. Can you clearly show each person how his or her particular job makes a difference?
- **Connect people to their teammates.** Engage your people by explaining the connection between what they do and their team's performance. Get everyone on the same side, pulling in their own unique way.
- **Communicate and involve people.** People can't support what they don't understand. Share all the information about goals and progress every step of the way.

WHO'S IN CHARGE HERE?

In Tysons Corner, Virginia, The Ritz-Carlton Hotel developed a new way to manage its business, taking teamwork, communication, and synergy to new levels. Called the "Tysons Project," the hotel drastically reduced the number of managers and created self-directed teams—frontline, hourly employees who run their own departments.

What happened? Productivity and profitability increased and turnover dropped 50 percent. Customer and employee satisfaction scores went from next-to-last in the company to number two worldwide.

Self-direction transfers the power and responsibility of managers into the hands of frontline employees. "As soon as we got to make decisions, we did all the things we knew we should have been doing all along," says

Steven Rauscher, a bartender in the front lounge. "The first thing we did was remove some of the beers that the managers always ordered but that we knew customers never wanted. Then we started buying single-malt scotches and different bourbons that guests had been asking for. The managers didn't even have a clue about that stuff.

> *Knowledge is power and knowledge shared is power multiplied.*
>
> —BOB NOYCE, cofounder of Intel, co-inventor of the integrated circuit, and first CEO of SEMATECH

"We do fine without a leader. But sometimes customers still want to speak to a manager. At first, we tried to explain that we're all in charge, but they couldn't comprehend that. So the team ordered business cards for everyone that say 'Manager' on them. Now, when a customer wants to speak to a manager, one of us can hand them our card and say, 'I'm the manager. Can I help you?'"

"I knew things were different when my team and I started doing our own payroll," remembers Wendy Watson, guest recognition coordinator. "We discipline our own teammates and do our own peer reviews and scheduling. We've been hired to do a job and we're trusted to do that job. I'm learning new skills and my mind has opened so much more. I'm educated and empowered."

WIN THEIR DISCRETIONARY EFFORT

For The Ritz-Carlton, self-direction was a natural choice. "We are switching from a management paradigm that is based on control and compliance to a commitment-based paradigm," explains Larry Sternberg, the mastermind behind the Tysons Project. "People do what they are supposed to do because they are committed to doing it and want to do it, not because we are ordering them to do it. The employee takes direction from the customer and the work process itself, not from a boss."

To many organizations this sounds much too frightening. What about all the mistakes that will happen? "Mistakes also happened when managers were around, I seem to recall," retorts Larry. "With self-direction, when an employee's decision turns out to be a bad one, they learn right away what to do next time because they own that decision. When a chef is sent a menu from the corporate office, what level of commitment can the chef have? If the menu fails, it's not his fault. But my restaurant team is committed. Its members go to competing restaurants in their free time and come back with reports and ideas to make their own menu the best it can be."

The Ritz-Carlton at Tysons Corner wins its people's "discretionary effort." "All people have discretionary effort," says Larry. "At most jobs, people give only what they have to in order to get the job done. They save their discretionary effort for things they really care about. Self-direction has tapped a tremendous amount of discretionary effort because people have psychological ownership of what happens in their department—they really care about what they do."

Self-direction also creates what Larry calls an "upward cascade." Supervisors used to have numerous, time-consuming tasks like scheduling, payroll, hiring, and training. But now they hand off those tasks to hourly employees. Supervisors can devote their time and expertise to planning that was normally reserved for department heads. Department heads now have time to focus on developing their business, coaching their people, and building customer relationships.

> We participate and interact, therefore we are.
>
> —JOHN SEELY BROWN, Chief Scientist, Xerox

"Throughout the centuries great products and services were actually planned and developed by frontline people," says Pat Mene, vice president. "Our forefathers planned, made, and sold their own products. Our company's move to self-direction is simply a return to this tradition—frontline workers planning, making decisions, and executing."

LEARN BY DOING

Corporate headquarters is excited about the Tysons Project and is rolling out self-direction worldwide. Consequently, Ritz-Carlton hotels are calling Tysons Corner for the blueprint on how it's accomplished. "Everybody's looking for the quick answer," says Steven Freund, food and beverage director. "They want a copy of the two-page, ten-step process. But we were ultimately successful precisely because we went through the discovery and learning process by ourselves with no rule books."

Employees agree that a significant cultural change must precede any physical changes. The hotel trusted, trained, and supported employees long before it implemented self-direction. As one frontline employee advised in true executive style, "Don't just take your managers out and say, 'OK, you're self-directed now.' You can't have that kind of chaos. We're still running a business here!"

Tysons Corner is full of turned-on people who act like they run the place—because they do. Employees love their work and customers see the difference. But Larry says the best is yet to come. "Pretty soon our people will have grown up under self-direction and they won't know any other way. It's like a country with an emerging democracy. Right after independence people struggle with how to do it. There's a lot of inefficiency, pain, and ambiguity. But as soon as there is a generation that is born and raised in it, they take it to a whole new level."

A WELL-EXECUTED BALLET

Like the employees at Tysons Corner, the 650 people associated with Mid-Columbia Medical Center have a deep, personal commitment to what they do. Everyone—from the janitor to the doctor—has a crucial role to play in making patient-centered care a reality. Even patients and their families are considered part of the team.

Nurse Sue Kelly remembers what it was like before the team saw the big picture. "It was always a power struggle—

family versus nurse, nurse versus doctor, patient versus nurse. Today it's like a well-executed ballet. Power isn't fought over, it is merged. Energies aren't dissipated in anger, they are blended."

Patients feel the difference team cohesiveness makes. "A patient who spent three weeks here wrote us a letter when he got back home," says Sue Kelly. "In it he not only thanks the doctors and the nurses, but he thanks the housekeepers, the kitchen help, the people that delivered the trays, and the people that rang up his food in the cafeteria—he even thanks the anesthetist. He recognized that every single person at the hospital was caring for him, not just the doctors and nurses."

People have individual responsibilities at Mid-Columbia, but caring for the patient is part of everybody's job description. In most hospitals, making a special request is no more than wishful thinking. But at Mid-Columbia special requests are a specialty. "We have a culture of teamwork that lets us care for our patients in a way that exceeds their expectations," says Randy Carter, administrative director of Mid-Columbia University. "A lab technician who gets a customer request can pick up any phone, call housekeeping, and say, 'Mr. Smith in room 332 wants a softer pillow and I promised it to him in fifteen minutes.' Now, the person he's talking to may already have a million things to do, but the patient's needs are paramount. The person in housekeeping delivers a soft pillow to Mr. Smith in five minutes, and we look like absolute superstars."

People at Mid-Columbia see the big picture. They

understand what it means to be teammates. "We all appreciate our connection to each other and the role played by each person," says Nurse Kelly. "I'm a nurse, not a housekeeper. But when I walk down a hall and see something on the floor, I pick it up. I don't say, 'What's the matter with those people in housekeeping?' I have a deep appreciation for what they do. I know that they are my partners. Sometimes a housekeeper will tell me, 'I was mopping the floor in room 212 and Mrs. Dodd doesn't look very alert today.' Her job isn't just to mop the floor. She has the same job as me—to take care of the patient."

When individuals come together and channel their energy, their efforts become a well-executed ballet. Communication creates a shared understanding and trust makes everyone feel like part of the team. People connected in a meaningful way and focused on a common purpose become an unstoppable force.

INSIGHT TO ACTION

Insight 7: Unleash the Power of People

Build a Winning Team

❑ Evaluate your teams. Be sure you have people who bring fresh perspectives and are willing to take action.

❑ Create a self-directed team in one or two areas.

- Define team objectives.
- Clarify roles, responsibilities, and boundaries.
- Agree on team processes.
- Decide on a method to track results.

❑ At your next meeting, have teams share how they are streamlining the business, meeting people/customer/profit goals, and what barriers are in the way. Find ways to remove barriers. Accelerate the process.

❑ Plan a relationship building day so your customers and people can work side by side on a community project such as Habitat for Humanity.

207

Practice 25

Learn by Design

The challenge is to regain our childhood curiosity and thirst for learning. We were really interesting at age four, pretty interesting at age seven and phenomenally boring at age thirty-five—let alone at fifty-one . . .

—TOM PETERS

As kids we loved learning new things. We couldn't wait to find out how stuff worked. We collaborated with our friends to invent new games. We looked forward to each day as an opportunity to explore new possibilities. And then something happened—we went first to school and then to work.

How have we managed to stifle that childhood curiosity and camaraderie? Roger's daughter Devon told him about a problem at school. Her fourth-grade class was assigned to do a report on the people, sports, hobbies, and businesses of Japan. Devon and three of her friends asked their teacher if they could combine their efforts, each of them writing about one of the areas. Her teacher said no, that it would be cheating. She said, "Dad, we can do a lot better job by working together . . . How come working together is cheating?"

Organizations need to take a hard look at their beliefs and assumptions about learning. Does your organization encourage collaboration and learning in the most effective way possible? "Learning organizations are distinguished by the ability to look at themselves," says SMU professor and author Mick McGill. "They think about getting smarter and unlearning—setting aside those things that no longer work for them."

> To gain knowledge, add something every day. To gain wisdom, get rid of something every day.
>
> —LAO TZU

Learning is a challenge for organizations today. How do you create a consistency of experience for all employees, full- and part-timers, who are often in widespread locations? The goal is to provide continuous learning opportunities that enhance people's personal growth and understanding of the business.

- **Provide "just in time" learning.** Create an urgency for learning. Deliver training and coaching as close as possible to the time it's needed.
- **Don't spray and pray.** Don't spray out a multitude of training programs and pray that your people will get what they need. Tailor learning around individual, team, and company needs. Provide growth opportunities that are flexible and dynamic to harness your people's talent and diversity.

- **Real time/real world.** Use every day as an opportunity for learning. Use your best people as mentors, coaches, and trainers. Focus on results—training must be hands-on, addressing real challenges. Set the tone by setting clear expectations about learning during the interview process.
- **Don't leave training to the training department.** It's everyone's job.

PROVIDE "JUST IN TIME" LEARNING

Trying to get people to learn something before they want it or need it is a waste of your money and their time. David Pottruck, president and COO of Charles Schwab, decided to create the want and the need. For years David had been trying to help Schwab's regional managers develop leadership skills. Each regional manager was responsible for about fourteen branches—a fair amount, but still manageable. And that was the problem: managers literally *managed* branches, watching their every move and making decisions for them.

With Schwab's projected growth rate of a compounded 20 percent per year, regional managers couldn't continue to successfully supervise the details. Branches had to manage themselves, but regional managers didn't want to give up control.

"So we cut the number of regional managers to ten," David explains . . .

. . . and made each responsible for twenty-five to thirty branches hundreds of miles apart—an *unmanageable* situation. And that's exactly the point. They can't manage every detail anymore; they can only lead. The only choice they have is to empower their branches and then trust and guide.

And we're going through some hell right now, struggling a bit as a result. But if you teach someone to lead who doesn't need to, they're not going to pay attention. People could care less about swimming when they're riding a bike. But you throw someone in the deep end and suddenly their interest in swimming becomes much greater. Now we have people screaming for leadership training, screaming for empowerment training, screaming for measurement systems to measure the effective use of that new empowerment. The key is to be ready with the training and the tools—the life preserver—when they start floundering.

Provide the tools and knowledge when there's an urgency to learn. If there's a need but no urgency, you may just want to create some.

DON'T SPRAY AND PRAY

Imagine having a new workforce every two years, with people from diverse companies and cultures. That's exactly the training dilemma faced at SEMATECH, the semiconductor manufacturing consortium. CEO Bill Spencer says that a standard curriculum for training and

211

development is useless. "We've got to have training resources that are available on demand, for whatever people need right now. People have got to be simultaneously eating while riding the chairlift or they're going to miss the next run."

SEMATECH created an innovative training process called Learning by Design—a flexible learning tool designed to educate new and current people about SEMATECH business priorities and values. The learning program emphasizes:

- **Needs-based learning.** Design ongoing learning to meet individual and company needs.
- **Responsibility.** Everyone is both a teacher and a learner.
- **Accountability.** Assume accountability for your own personal and professional growth.
- **Broad-based learning.** Create a variety of learning experiences, formats, and locations.
- **Multiple Perspectives.** See how other people run their businesses and their lives.
- **Results-based learning.** Tie compensation to learning.
- **Downloading.** Unlearn what no longer works.

SEMATECH's Learning by Design is a learning laboratory that coordinates ongoing seminars and meetings while researching the best available learning resources. Used as an effective tool to achieve SEMATECH goals, this unique learning process provides personalized coaching and tools to address a rapidly changing team and each individual's requirements.

REAL TIME/REAL WORLD

The San Antonio River Center Marriott trains its people exactly as it wants them to perform—hands-on when it comes to guests and hands-off when it comes to rules and regulations. The hands-on training begins during the interview process. Applicants work at different stations in the hotel, including the front desk, concierge desk, and bell stand, before being hired. Applicants are shadowed by an associate who notes how they handle themselves, how personal they are with guests, and how well they build rapport.

The orientation process for new workers at the River Center Marriott is a series of meetings and on-the-job coaching over the first sixty days of employment. The first day on the job is spent

> Managers should be students of their business. The more you know, the better you will perform.
>
> —BILL MARRIOTT, Chairman and President, Marriott International

learning about the principles of hospitality and problem-solving techniques. But after that, the hotel lets people do what they feel is necessary to make sure "every guest leaves satisfied."

"For the first few months, Wendy Jarvis was my coach,"

says Computer Systems Administrator Jake Farmer. "We would talk each day about things that came up—situations I felt uncomfortable with or things I felt I could've handled better. We discussed what I was learning as I experienced things. Being oriented as I worked was very concrete and meaningful."

"It's really important to stay close to new people during the first two months," adds Wendy. "That's when they're most nervous and unsure of themselves. We don't want to lose good people because we didn't help them when they first came on board."

A mentored, hands-on approach to training helps the San Antonio River Center Marriott post associate and customer satisfaction scores that are consistently among the highest in the chain. Are you losing good people in their first sixty days?

DON'T LEAVE TRAINING TO THE TRAINING DEPARTMENT

Worlds away from luxury hotels, inner-city communities discovered that learning is too important to be solely in the hands of a "training department." The successful turnaround of Coliseum Gardens, for example, all started when the decision-making power was given to the people closest to the problems—the residents. The success story continues even though the Health Realization "trainers" are gone because the ability to change comes directly from the residents themselves.

"I worked in one community for three or four years," says Beverley Wilson, Health Realization trainer. "When my partner and I left, all of the work we had done left, too. That hurt me to the core of my heart. I asked myself, 'Why didn't the people keep going with it?' Well, now I know the reason. They didn't run with it because we made it seem like the reason it was working was because we were doing it for them. *We brought it to them, instead of letting it come from within themselves.* It's the same old parable. You can give people fish and feed them for a day. That's what most programs do. But if you can teach them to fish and they can own it and feel it inside, then they will eat for a lifetime."

Roger Mills, president of the Health Realization Institute, acknowledges that the goal is to eliminate rigid processes and the notion of "fixing people." "I can come in and show them a few things, but they move it along much further than I ever could because they own it and develop it. If I told them, 'In order to succeed, you must do Step A, then Step B, then Step C,' they'd be stuck on getting Step B perfectly right instead of using their own wisdom to come up with the solutions."

Do people dread your training courses? It doesn't have to be that way. Start right away, first creating an urgency for continuous growth and learning, then offering the right tools at the right time. Make it real-world and meaningful, and let people design learning that is best for them—the way you learned when you were a child.

INSIGHT TO ACTION

Insight 7: Unleash the Power of People

Learn by Design

❑ Put together a comprehensive sixty-day orientation process for new people.

- Start with the hiring process.
- Use your best people as mentors and coaches.

❑ Identify ways to include learning as an integral part of all meetings, site visits, and company events.

❑ Make a personal learning goal part of everyone's objectives.

❑ Identify three things to *unlearn*. Get rid of assumptions that no longer apply (e.g., all learning takes place in the classroom).

- _____

- _____

- _____

❑ Don't leave training up to the trainers. Involve your best people—senior management, star performers, and line associates.

Practice 26

Put Your Money
Where Your Mouth Is

It's very important to incent people for what they have control over. I'm on the board of a few companies, and I hear a lot of people say, "We are going to reward people based on our stock price." Well, there's absolutely no connection between what a frontline person does today and what the stock price is going to be tomorrow. You can't incent people for things they have no control over. It's not only ineffective, it's counterproductive.

—CHUCK SCHWAB,
Chairman and CEO,
Charles Schwab Corporation

When a chain of restaurants couldn't figure out why its customer counts and satisfaction were dropping so quickly, Sue was called in to investigate. Management said it always stressed the importance of pleasing the customer. But when Sue looked into the compensation program, she found the problem. Executive chefs and managers were paid year-end bonuses based on profits, so they were ruthlessly raising prices and reducing food and labor costs. The company was caught in a customer satisfaction death spiral—higher menu prices and fewer people serving customers smaller portions of food. Sue worked with the chain to include a customer satisfaction and value component to the incentive program. Not surprisingly, the change prompted creativity in purchasing and preparing food and restored customer counts and satisfaction.

People do what they're paid for. Put your money where your mouth is.

- **Compensate for what you care about.**
- **Reward people only for what they have control over.**
- **Keep incentive programs clear and simple.**

AN AMAZING FINDING

Chuck Schwab, frustrated by the intimidating sales pressure of large brokerage houses, founded his company vowing to be the best at serving customers at an affordable price. He still looks at everything through the eyes of a client, asking "How will this affect our customer?" before making any decision.

A lot of companies say the same thing, but a lot of companies aren't number one in their industry for customer service. So how does Charles Schwab make good on all that talk? It puts its money where its mouth is.

Since 1985 Charles Schwab has surveyed its customers regarding the service they receive on a frequent and systematic basis. Every night, surveys for a random sample of the day's transactions are sent out. Each questionnaire notes the specific transaction and the Schwab employee who handled it.

> *Where else would a vice president teach you everything he knows and not get jealous when you make more money than he does?*
>
> —MARY KAY
> SALES ASSOCIATE

Bill Baughman recently came to Schwab from one of its major competitors. As senior vice president of strategic marketing in charge of the customer survey program, he's still in awe of how well Schwab backs up its commitment to the customer. "Our service quality people send out over 3,000 questionnaires every night for trades, sales inquiries, account maintenance, and branch visits—a whole range of interactions. There's a customer satisfaction index score published every week for all to see."

Schwab ensures top-notch customer service because it ties the survey results directly to the compensation of each employee. At the end of every quarter, frontline reps are paid a bonus based on the scores their specific customers gave them. "Employees must always think about our values and how we want to treat our customers," says Chuck

219

Schwab. "So we let the customers vote, and reward people based on each customer's level of satisfaction. People tend to do what they get rewarded for—amazing finding, isn't it?"

YOU GET WHAT YOU PAY FOR

Every day at Intel is fast, furious, and competitive. But January through April the intensity is turned up a few more notches. It's ranking and rating season again, when bonuses and salary increases are determined for all 43,000 employees worldwide.

Intel demands continuous learning, growth, and improvement, and compensates its people accordingly. The ranking and rating process compares how well individuals perform relative to their peers in similar posts throughout the company.

A ranking and rating session includes ten to fifteen managers, each representing their direct reports. Managers come to the session with all the pertinent information about each employee's performance, including her major accomplishments and comments from the employee and her peers, subordinates, and customers.

In the session, managers give each person two ratings. The first denotes an individual's performance for the year on the corporate objectives—outstanding, good, or poor. The second evaluates a person's development as compared to her peers. Again, there are three possible ratings:

- **Faster than.** Develops and applies skills more quickly than her peers; ready for more responsibility.
- **Equal to.** Doing a good job and maintaining average growth.
- **Slower than.** Peers are progressing more quickly.

An employee can receive a "good" performance rating on the annual objectives, but if her peers performed equally well, she is alerted to pick up the pace.

When the managers reach consensus on each rating, they rank the entire group into tiers—a top third, a middle third, and a bottom third. Each person's year-end bonus and new salary is then calculated on the spot.

Intel pays for learning, growth, and improvement—and that's exactly what it gets.

PARTNERS IN PERFORMANCE

Levi Strauss & Co.'s phenomenal 60 percent growth in revenue and whopping 175 percent increase in income over the last five years is due in large part to its clear alignment. Levi Strauss & Co. has a clear picture of what it wants to be and how it wants to work, exemplified by its Aspirations Statement of company values. The Aspirations pledge a commitment to teamwork, diversity, recognition, ethical management practice, communication, and empowerment. The company also emphasizes its long-term strategic objectives. But prior to 1992, Levi Strauss &

Co. employees received incentives based only on how well they fulfilled their job descriptions. Realizing that any compensation program must be aligned with its Aspirations and long-term goals, Levi Strauss & Co. put together a team of executives, managers, and associates to rebuild the entire system. The result is Partners in Performance.

The new system eliminates the disconnect between what the company cares about and what it pays people to do. "Partners in Performance was created by employees for employees," explains Jann Westfal, president of the company's Slates brand. "It's a powerful force because it's more than a compensation package. Partners in Performance integrates business management, people management, our Aspirations, and our long-term objectives. People are now paid for working on the right things in the right way."

Under the new plan, Levi Strauss & Co. rewards associates for their individual and team achievements in four areas:

- Annual business objectives
- Long-range strategic objectives
- Aspirations
- Continuous growth and improvement

At the beginning of the year, with these four categories in mind, managers meet with each direct report and establish five to eight personal objectives. There is mutual accountability—both the manager and the employee are responsible for hitting the targets.

Mid-year, the manager and associate talk about how well the personal objectives are being met and whether the targets need to be altered in light of any new developments.

At year end, people are eligible for a bonus based on their performance. After three years of dedication to the Aspirations, business and long-term objectives, and continuous growth, associates receive a long-term incentive award.

Partners in Performance finally aligned where Levi Strauss & Co. wants to go with what its people are doing to get there. "The message to our people is clear: it's not acceptable to achieve your financial objectives if, in the process, you violate our Aspirations," says Tom Kasten. "Our strategic and business objectives describe *what* we want to accomplish and our Aspirations describe *how* we want to go about it. They're both important, and we finally have a system that rewards people for doing both."

INSIGHT TO ACTION

Insight 7: Unleash the Power of People

Put Your Money Where Your Mouth Is

❑ List your top three:

Company Priorities	Compensation Criteria
_____	_____
_____	_____
_____	_____

❑ Are the answers in both columns identical? If not, rethink your compensation program—it will never get you where you want to go.

❑ Reality check: Ask five people in your organization to do the same. Does their reality match your reality?

Practice 27

Make Every Person Feel Special

I played football in college. I wasn't very big—only 150 pounds—and I wasn't very good. I got hurt a lot. I broke my arm once, my neck once, and my nose six times. When I tell people about it, they always ask me, 'Why did you keep doing it?' For the longest time I had no answer. Then one day it hit me. If there hadn't been any fans in the stands cheering me on—my family and friends—I wouldn't have kept on playing and trying so hard. But there were, so I did.

—TOM MALONE
President, Milliken &
Company

Tom Malone endured hours of practice and played his heart out every Saturday simply because people were watching and he wanted to be recognized. We all need praise and recognition. There's something inside that makes us try new things and perform better than we ever thought we could if someone is paying attention. It was true when we shouted, "Look Ma, no hands!" It was true when we went out for the team even though we got clobbered. And it's true today in the world of business.

Money is a powerful incentive—it will help get people to do what you want—but money does nothing to stoke a person's internal fire. Enduring motivation comes from inside, and heartfelt recognition gets it going. When you give sincere praise, you connect with people emotionally—they work harder because they want to, not because you pay them to.

- **Recognize what's important.** What gets recognized gets attention and effort. Don't send mixed messages.
- **Give formal and informal recognition.** Formal recognition is regular and expected. Informal recognition is more personal, happens on the spot, and is many times more meaningful.
- **Make it personal.** Each person wants to be recognized differently. Find out how and tailor your recognition.

THE BEST VALUES IN TOWN

In 1991 Intel invented a way to celebrate its corporate values. It's called the Intel Quality Award, which even Dave

Crowley, who's responsible for the award, agrees is a bit of a misnomer. "It really should be the Intel Values Award, because quality is just one of our values."

The Intel Quality Award recognizes departments that excel at Intel values. The application has six sections, each representing a different value. Business units that apply for the award document their performance on:

- Results orientation
- Quality
- Discipline
- Great place to work
- Risk-taking
- Customer orientation

Departments that make the cut present their achievements to a special executive review team. An elite few are declared the winners.

> If anything goes bad, then I did it. If anything goes semi-good, then we did it. If anything goes real good, then you did it. That's all it takes to get people to win football games for you.
>
> —BEAR BRYANT

Although inspired by the Malcolm-Baldrige National Quality Award, Dave says the Intel Quality Award serves a slightly different purpose. "The award recognizes people for working with our values, but it also establishes a way for our business units to assess themselves and improve their performance against those values. The Baldrige award is an excellent way to evaluate the systems and processes of an organization. For the Intel environment, the Intel values are much more important. They tell us how to make our organization run at a peak level of efficiency."

Winning organizations are surrounded by an aura of prestige. "We position it as the highest level of recognition Intel can bestow on a division, department, or team," explains Dave. "There's a certain attraction in showcasing your achievements in front of senior management. So the award is on people's agendas. They know that living by Intel values leads to recognition and distinction."

The Intel Quality Award is building momentum. Only twelve groups applied in its first year. Today over two-thirds of the business units at Intel have gone through the award process. Winners become Intel celebrities and share the secret of their success with aspiring departments. "The coaching and mentoring that goes on from year to year accelerates the transfer of the best methods throughout the company on an informal basis," says Dave.

Intel's use of formal recognition elevates the importance of its values and sends a clear message that how the company does business is just as important as what it does.

MR. MARRIOTT IS ON THE PHONE . . .

Formal awards spur momentum in an organization, but informal recognition is much more meaningful to individuals. Every month Bill Marriott personally calls the company's top six sales people—those who exceed their goal by the largest percentage. "I really look forward to making those calls," says Bill. "Most of the time I'm on the phone trying to solve problems. Calling these young salespeople is a lot more fun. Besides, is there a better use of my time than thanking our people for their great efforts?"

Calls from Mr. Marriott himself are treasured by the recipients and talked about for months afterward, but sometimes Bill has difficulty convincing people that it's really him on the phone. "Sure you are, and I'm Leona Helmsley," replied one woman, certain a colleague was playing a prank.

> The words "innovative" and "creative" have been used to describe us. It's embarrassing that it's innovative or creative to treat people with respect and dignity.
>
> —JACQUE SCOTT,
> Administrative
> Director of
> Nursing Services,
> Mid-Columbia
> Medical Center

Marriott's president, executive vice president, and vice president of sales also call six leading performers each month. What would it take for you to do the same thing?

Tom Chase is the general manager of the Minneapolis City Center Marriott—a perennial associate and customer satisfaction leader. How does he build morale and a passion to serve the customer? Recognition. Each week he writes ten letters to people who've been singled out by guests or fellow associates for a job well done. "You can't imagine how important those are," Tom says. "I send the letters to their homes so that they can open them in front of their families. Most of those letters are displayed on the most revered spot in the home—the refrigerator door."

You don't have to be a big spender to have a big effect on your people. You can get a tremendous amount of mileage out of a phone call or a postage stamp.

PRAISE PEOPLE TO SUCCESS

Mary Kay Cosmetics is well-known for the material rewards offered to its salespeople—pink Cadillacs, pearl necklaces, and diamond jewelry. But the most powerful motivator for Mary Kay consultants is not the glittering prizes but personal recognition. Formal events like Seminar figure prominently, but informal recognition inspires the sales force to success. That inspiration generated $1.7 billion in retail sales in 1995.

The company sends out 450,000 birthday, holiday, and anniversary cards every year, and Mary Kay Ash praises high achievers personally. "Whenever people do something extraordinary, their director is supposed to let me know about it," she says. "I send each of them a handwritten note saying, 'I heard about what you did, and I thank you from the bottom of my heart for being so thoughtful.' They frame those notes for family and friends to see because it makes them feel happy, needed, and important. They work harder because I wrote two or three little sentences on a piece of paper."

At a weekly sales meeting, Kathy Helou shared her success story with the group. "I've won six cars and lots of diamonds. But this note is my most treasured possession." She proceeded to unfold a tattered, faded piece of paper which she read aloud, tears welling in her eyes. "'You did a great job this week. I knew you could do it!' Signed, Mary Kay Ash. I still remember the day I received this. I said to myself, 'Kathy you *can* do it. You can go all the way!'" And she did.

Recognition goes right down to the local level where sales directors are encouraged to give whatever kind of recognition or prize that would be most meaningful to each of their people. Heartfelt recognition can come anytime, for anything.

At Mary Kay people work hard for the honor of wearing their red jackets at weekly sales meetings or a chance to sit at the head of the table at the next Star Consultant Night. Women set sales records to get their names on a birthday card to Mary Kay Ash.

"We had one contest called the 20/20 Club," remembers Rhonda Shasteen. "If any consultant held twenty skin care classes in one month, she'd be called onstage at our Career Conference to receive a ribbon personally signed by Mary Kay Ash. What does a ribbon cost? A nickel. What does the onstage recognition cost? Nothing. Yet that contest created so much excitement, sales, and profits, it's just phenomenal."

Does praise only work for women? Would men rather take the money and run? Mark Scott exploded that myth. The CEO sent some information about Mid-Columbia

Medical Center to Mary Kay Ash and in return received a handwritten note praising him for the outstanding and important job that he does. "It was a very touching letter from Mary Kay Ash," says Mark. "A great letter. In fact, I framed it and put it up right here in my office."

Mary Kay Cosmetics proves you can praise people to success. High-tech employees, hotel employees, even CEOs all push a little harder for a pat on the back.

INSIGHT TO ACTION

Insight 7: Unleash the Power of People

Make Every Person Feel Special

❑ Remember the last Insight to Action, Put Your Money Where Your Mouth Is? Add a third column: your "Top three recognition criteria." Make sure all three columns are aligned.

Top three company priorities	Top three compensation criteria	Top three recognition criteria
_____	_____	_____
_____	_____	_____
_____	_____	_____

❑ Has anyone ever complained about being recognized for a job well done?

- Do more of it.
- Make recognition a part of your daily life.

❑ Each month:

- Send ten personal thank-you notes to people's homes.
- Call and thank five star performers.

Practice 28

The Power of One

"This year's award for the best sports salesperson in all of Marriott goes to . . . Albert 'Smitty' Smith! Come on up here, Smitty!"

An unknown gentleman came up from the back of the room. He was impeccably dressed in a tuxedo and white gloves, and covered from head to toe with pins, buttons, and medals of dazzling variety. He accepted his award, then stepped to the microphone nervously.

You've probably guessed that I'm not a salesperson like all of you. I don't have business cards and an office—I'm a room service captain at the Atlanta Marriott. What I do have is a relationship with all the sports teams. When a team comes to town, I work twenty-four hours a day to take care of their every wish. I know what every player, every coach, and every manager likes as their special order. Sometimes they even call me before they get to town and request special snacks and treats.

Last year, a competing hotel offered rooms to teams for four dollars less than we were charging. Half the teams went to that hotel to take advantage of the lower prices. Whenever a team that wasn't staying at the Marriott came to town, I took the day off. I'd call one of my friends at the other hotel to find out what time the team was scheduled to arrive. Then I'd go over in full uniform and wait for the team in the lobby.

One time, the Dodgers came to town. Tommy Lasorda led the team into the competing hotel, and I was standing there waiting for him. Tommy smiled, shook my hand, and said, "Smitty, what are you doing here? Are you with this hotel now? This is great! So are we."

"No, I'm still at the Marriott."

"What are you doing here, then?"

"Well, I just wanted to welcome you to town, wish you good luck against the Braves, and tell you that I'm bringing over your special order from Marriott after the game tonight."

He asked me why I would do such a thing, and I told him that first of all, his new hotel's room service closes at eleven P.M.—if the game went extra innings, he'd miss his late night snack. "But more importantly," I said, "I just want you to know that even though you can't afford to stay with us anymore, we still love you."

Smitty went on to say that the Dodgers, and every other team that left, came back to Marriott the very next year.

Something amazing happens when people feel both a deep commitment to the work they do and a responsibility for their sphere of influence—they discover they have the power to do the extraordinary. They are turned on! The

235

power of one is strong—and contagious. It lies within each of us. All it takes is one person, one day, to make a difference.

COMMITMENT TO CARING

When patient-centered care was introduced at Harbor Hospital, Nurse Michelle Pitter-Jones was the biggest cynic—hard to believe when you learn that she was recently voted Nurse of the Year. "I've had to work my whole nursing career with a million things that all need attention at the same time," says Michelle. "I had to cut myself up into so many pieces I could never give all of me to one person. I felt guilty every day because I wasn't able to perform the way I could. I told my boss all the time, 'This nursing thing, there's got to be a better way to do it.' And I'm sure glad that better way came, because I was finished, burned out beyond belief. Now I'm refreshed. I have new hope."

> Will our leaders, structure, and culture allow our people to give their intellects and their hearts to our company? Ultimately, that's all that matters.
>
> —CARL SEWELL,
> President,
> Sewell Motor
> Company

Michelle's friendly voice can be heard throughout the floor. Patients ask for her by name, and she likes being the

236

nurse they feel most comfortable with. She spends time with each of her new patients to build trust and rapport. "When I know them as human beings, I learn what special things I can do to get them well and home to their families faster. I only hope that one day, if and when I'm in a hospital, there'll be a person who wants to care as much for me as I do for my patients."

Not only does Michelle care deeply about her patients, she keeps patient-centered care on track for the whole floor. Whenever she hears coworkers complaining or slipping into the "old way" by talking down to people, Michelle is always the first to speak up. "I simply remind them that we all signed a commitment. Then I say, 'We're here working together, so what can I do to help you?' First they look at me like I'm crazy—it's a real mindblower when people realize that someone is willing to help—and then they understand. 'Well, could you help me do this? I just have too much to do all at once.' I say, 'Sure. Let's just relax and do it together and everything will get done.'"

PEACE, FOR A CHANGE

Vivian Jefferson is a slight woman with graying hair, an expressive face, and a soft, mothering voice. She's a paid staff member of Coliseum Gardens, her residence for many years, and a Health Realization teacher for the community.

Five years ago she felt an overwhelming hopelessness.

She worried about her nine children and nineteen grand-children. She worried about her finances and the increasingly desperate community in which she lived. Two of her daughters struggled with crack cocaine addictions, and Vivian took over the raising of their children. Like others in the community, she felt life was out of her control.

Vivian was skeptical of the new community empowerment program, but she and a few of her neighbors gave it a try. The group began meeting regularly. It outlined much-needed improvements—everything from more activities for children to replacing the streetlights shot out by drug dealers.

Perhaps only that small group remembers the feeling of triumph the day those lights finally came back on. But no one in Coliseum Gardens will ever forget the day a riot *didn't* break out when the police arrested somebody.

During a meeting, Vivian and her partners heard the familiar sound of a riot in the making. They raced outside to see what the problem was this time. The police had just handcuffed a young boy that everyone knew and were escorting him to the squad car when the group arrived.

Vivian fought her way through the crowd to the line of heavily armed police officers.

> *The single most positive thing a person can do for herself is to set her own goal. When you own your goal, you find that nighttime usually interrupts all the things you want to do.*
>
> —KATHY HELOU,
> National Sales Director,
> Mary Kay Cosmetics

238

"What did he do?" she asked one officer.

The officer explained that the police keep tabs on who comes in and out of the complex to make sure they aren't drug dealers. They stop everyone and ask to see some ID. This boy had refused and tried to start a fight.

Vivian went to the police car where the boy sat sullenly. "What's going on? What did you do?"

"I didn't do anything! They stopped me for no reason. He just told me I had to give him my wallet."

"Well, actually they did stop you for a reason. Their job is to protect our community from the drug dealers. They asked for your ID to make sure you belonged in here. Why did you start to fight?"

"When the officer grabbed me and cuffed me, he broke the new watch I got for Christmas. I was just mad."

Vivian went back to the police and told them the boy's story. "You didn't explain to him why you wanted his ID. And you obviously handled him a bit rough, because you did break his watch."

The officers thought about it and took the cuffs off the boy. They'd see what they could do about the broken watch. And it just stopped right there. No bottles were thrown. No riot gear was needed. The crowd turned around and walked away. A week later, the officers gave the boy a new watch just like the one before.

Vivian's heroic effort ended the stalemate between the police and the community, creating a new era of communication and cooperation. Both sides began to talk to each other and see things from the other's perspective. Vivian says that her courage came from the classes she'd been taking. No matter. It was one person, one day, who was sick and tired of the same old thing and wanted to make a difference.

Your organization is full of people with the courage of Vivian Jefferson, the soul of Michelle Pitter-Jones, and the tenacity of "Smitty" Smith. They are just waiting to make a difference. Engage their hearts and minds. Give them the freedom to act.

Epilogue: The power of Smitty continued when the delegation from the city of Atlanta went to Seoul and Tokyo to bid for the 1996 Summer Olympic Games. The delegation included top political figures, corporate board directors—and Albert "Smitty" Smith. "They made a bunch of presentations to the decision committee," he says of the delegates. "That was nice and all, but during the breaks I talked with the committee about what the people of Atlanta are really like. I told them about Georgia's hospitality and how much we love sports!" Of course, the committee awarded the Olympics to Atlanta. We weren't there, but knowing Smitty, we bet his personal commitment and pride in Atlanta pushed it over the top . . .

INSIGHT TO ACTION

Insight 7: Unleash the Power of People

The Power of One

❏ Actively seek out individuals who are making a difference in your company or your community.

❏ Find ways to tell one or two of their stories each month as an example of outstanding individual accomplishment.

❏ Set up a "Power of One" Hall of Fame with:

• Pictures on walls

• Articles in newsletters

• Celebrations at meetings

ENTHUSIASTIC CUSTOMERS

INSPIRED PEOPLE

FINANCIAL PERFORMANCE

8. Lead with Care

7. Unleash the Power of People

6. Measure Well, Act Fast

5. Make Technology Your Servant

4. Simplify, Simplify, Simplify

3. Have the Courage to Set Bold Goals

2. Make Every Customer Feel Special

1. Build a Strong Foundation

Insight 8

Lead with Care

Once again the wisdom of children gets straight to the heart of the matter. The clarity and purity of their words raises the question, "How do we make it so hard?" Our thanks to Abby, Allison, Brian, Eli, Jodi, Kate, Liam, and Zach—the leaders of tomorrow.

"WHAT DOES A LEADER DO?"

- *A leader is the one who makes you want to work hard and then makes you feel good because you did.*

- *When a bunch of people come together to do something, a leader is the one who finds out what everybody is good at and what they want to do. They take all that, then add some special something that makes the group do better than anyone could ever do by themselves.*

- *A leader is sometimes thought of as a mean, bossy person, but if they are doing it right, they should seem like a friend who wants to help you out.*

- *Sometimes you think you don't want to do something, but when a leader gets done with you, you are excited and can't wait to start!*

- *A good leader shouldn't be really nice when you are around, then be mean when you're not around. He should be the same no matter what he does—or she does.*

- *I think leaders should open their minds and listen to lots of new ideas—especially from the people they lead. Let other people have a chance, too.*

- *When you really help another person, you get a happy feeling that just takes you over. It makes you want to do even more helping.*

"WHY DOES A LEADER HAVE SUCH A HARD JOB?"

- *A leader is supposed to be the one who knows it all, but sometimes you feel like you don't know it all.*

You just have to be honest and tell people you need help. I think they'll understand.

- *If somebody wants to do a wonderful puppet show, you've got to encourage them and make them believe that they can do it. You have to really believe they can do it, though, or else they will be able to tell and think you're just saying that.*

- *When you mess up, just say you messed up. It's no big deal.*

- *You don't want to say, "Hey, I think you're doing a bad job" or anything. You've got encourage them, and then you've got to show them how to do better.*

- *I think you must be a little bit strict, a little bit strong, a little bit friendly, and a little bit encouraging. I think that's hard to be all at one time.*

THE ART OF LEADERSHIP

"Management still believes that leadership means telling people what to do," says Horst Schulze of The Ritz-Carlton. "Leadership to me is a very simple thing—creating consensus and aligning people behind a vision, not only by telling people what needs to be done but—and this is key—why it should be done. Creating an environment in which people *want* to do the job, rather than *have* to do the job—that is leadership."

Leadership drives an organization. Leaders set the standard for everybody with their words and actions. At the same time, they bring out the best in people and encourage individual strengths. Leaders are the ultimate source of inspiration and vision. Their integrity and strength of character captures the trust and dedication of their people. Leaders are great teachers and constant learners, always listening and seeking out new ideas.

The children above remind us that a leader must first be a person. "We're all just human beings who want to feel good about what we're doing," says Mary Kay's Kathy Helou. "If leaders could just let down their guard, have fun, and show that they are human beings, people would move mountains for them."

For centuries people have moved mountains for great leaders. Winston Churchill, Mother Teresa, and Martin Luther King had extraordinarily different styles. But each could rally people around a cause and inspire action. Who last inspired you—a teacher, a coach, a boss? No doubt they shared the same attributes of great leaders past, present, and future.

Leadership comes in all shapes and sizes. It's not a title that makes a leader, but attitude and commitment. Every organization has leaders at all levels. Whether in the executive office or on the front line, leaders are people who take pride in and responsibility for the work they do. They take charge of their own sphere of influence and see themselves as a resource to others—teaching, inspiring, and motivating whenever they can.

No matter who you are or what you do, you can be a leader. Set an example for others and build leaders all around you. Commit yourself to continuous learning and regularly renew both yourself and your work. Open your mind to new ideas and embrace the spirit of fun and adventure. And most important, don't be afraid to care deeply about the people you serve.

Practice 29 **GUARDIAN OF THE VALUES**

Practice 30 **PROMOTE LEADERSHIP AT ALL LEVELS**

Practice 31 **RENEW YOURSELF AND EVERYONE WINS**

Practice 32 **YOU MUST CARE**

Practice 29

Guardian of the Values

When all is said and done, more is said than done.

—Lou Holtz,
head football coach,
University of Notre Dame

What do you feel is important? What do you tell your people is important? What do you actually do? The leader of an organization is the guardian of its values, and actions speak louder than words. "Once you lie to somebody," says Jerry Williams, a community police officer in Oakland, California, "once you say one thing but do another—it's all over."

A leader's ability to live the values he or she espouses is critical not only for trust but for the survival of the values system itself. "What is missing in leadership today is follow through, follow through, follow through with integrity, integrity, integrity," says John O'Neil, president of the California School of Professional Psychology and author of *The Paradox of Success*. "Follow through without integrity does not work. People are terrified of one-night stands. Another broken promise, another broken heart. If leaders aren't willing to live their values, then people will never trust the leader or the values."

A LEGENDARY LEADER

Fourteen semiconductor companies originally agreed to partner under the umbrella of SEMATECH, but some did not send their best people to work there as promised.

SEMATECH's CEO, the late Bob Noyce, knew he couldn't invent the future without having the best talent on his team. He set an immediate precedent when he sent underqualified people right back to their respective companies. He called each member CEO and gave him a list of the people he expected instead. The word was out—SEMATECH was a serious venture and its success required the best everyone had to offer. Anything less was unacceptable.

At one meeting early in SEMATECH's history, the joint staff was discussing a plan to allocate resources. Miller Bonner, SEMATECH's director of communications, was in the room that day. "Andy Grove from Intel sat there and listened patiently for the whole meeting—which is quite long for Andy. Then he stood up and said, 'You know, I've been sitting here for two hours listening to this bullshit about all your fancy plans. The only thing on your agenda should be meeting Intel's needs because if you don't do

249

that, I'm out of here!' That started all the other company representatives, 'Yeah. Forget all this other stuff—you better get focused on us or else!'"

In actuality, says Miller, Bob staged this reality check with Andy Grove ahead of time. Bob understood that creating a sense of urgency sometimes requires the passionate words of a customer or supplier. In SEMATECH's case, Bob knew that Andy Grove had the respect of his peers and would tell it like it is in a way that would mobilize everyone to action.

SEMATECH got off to a strong start thanks to a great leader with clear values and the actions to back them up.

A SINGULARITY OF RHETORIC AND REALITY

In 1991 David Pottruck suggested that Chuck Schwab write a vision and values statement. "What do you mean?" Chuck replied. "Why would we have to write something down? Everybody who knows me understands what this company is all about."

And it's true—like Bob Noyce, Chuck lives and breathes his values. But with 6,500 Schwab employees across the nation, not everyone can see Chuck in action. He was convinced, and finally put to paper what had been driving the company for so long.

"That is pretty special," says Lindy Ashmore, director of corporate quality at Schwab. "Most companies do the opposite—they do market research to find out what their customers care about, then draft a values statement. But Chuck lived his values for twenty-four years before it dawned on him to write them down. Our values statement says, 'Fair, Empathetic, and Responsive,' and no three words could describe Chuck better."

David says Chuck's ability to tear himself away from the day-to-day business and spend meaningful time with customers reinforces the company's customer obsession. "In fact," says David, "he's more like a customer than one of us."

Chuck visits the branches constantly to talk with his people and holds town meeting Q & A sessions at headquarters. "Chuck has a personal relationship with 6,500 employees," says Vice-Chairman Larry Stupski. That personal relationship makes the values of Charles Schwab more than a piece of paper that's been around since 1991, but a way of life that's driven the company for twenty-four years.

"At Charles Schwab, the rhetoric and the reality are closer together than at any other company I know," says Bill Baughman, SVP of strategic marketing. "So close together, it's astounding." That's what great leadership is all about—a singularity of rhetoric and reality.

ACT LIKE A FAMILY—PARTICULARLY IN TOUGH TIMES

The values that Bill Marriott carefully guards for his organization are best summed in one word: *family*.

A large organization has to act like a family, particularly in tough times. When you care about people and their families, they know it and they'll be very loyal in return. I used to watch my dad go into a hotel. He'd talk sincerely with the people about what mattered to them. He'd stand in the laundry talking to a housekeeper, "How's your job? How's your family?" Those kind of things are the ultimate demonstration of caring.

When I go to a hotel, I talk to every single associate. I think the fact that you just say hello to them and recognize them puts caring into it. I don't believe I'm that important—but people ask to take a picture with me. They tell me they send them to their relatives or make copies to put in their homes. People want somebody to look up to and respect—I know I do.

One interviewer asked me if what we were doing was one of those California, touchy-feely kinds of things. I responded, "What part of 'respect' don't you understand? What is so radically wrong with our society when we can't raise ourselves to the level of treating patients, family members, and each other with respect and dignity?"

—MARK SCOTT,
CEO, Mid-Columbia
Medical Center

Bill says that values and a mission statement are very different. "I think your values are created by the style you portray in everything you do. In a mission statement you try to put it in words—but they're just words. So many CEOs and executives in today's world don't seem to care about people, and their people know it. That's just not the way you do business—not for long anyway."

252

Spend time with Bill Marriott and you see that he truly is the Guardian of the Values, backing up his words with every action.

KEEPER OF THE KARMA

Cole Hardware is not as well known as Charles Schwab, SEMATECH, or Marriott, but to the residents of San Francisco the name means quite a lot.

As soon as you walk in the door, a nostalgic, comfortable, wonderful feeling sweeps over you. "Even when I know I don't need anything," says one customer, "I like to go in and walk up and down the aisles. The place just feels good." Every customer who walks in, whether to feel good or to buy some nails, knows the owner, Rick Karp. Rick is as much a landmark in the community as his store. He's there every day of the week, talking to customers and working alongside the Cole Hardware staff.

The shop was handed down to Rick by his father. Rick is now the company's president—make that, former president. "I've never been comfortable with the title 'president,' it's just not me," he says. "What I really love to do, and what I hope I am known for, is working hard to keep the karma of Cole Hardware fresh and alive. There seems to be a feeling around Cole Hardware that I really can't describe. It comes from nurturing my people, both staff and customers. My real job is the best job in the world

253

when I come to think about it. I get to concentrate on making Cole Hardware the best place to work and to shop. I am the Keeper of the Karma."

Rick promptly changed his business cards to read, "The Keeper of the Karma." The words merely capture the essence of his leadership. His actions demonstrate what Cole Hardware is all about.

Bob Noyce, Chuck Schwab, Bill Marriott, and Rick Karp follow through with integrity. Their people and customers feel the sincerity and commitment in everything they do. They are Guardians of the Values.

INSIGHT TO ACTION

Insight 8: Lead with Care

Guardian of the Values

❑ Consistently do what you say you're going to do.

❑ Use all opportunities to showcase stories that exemplify your values. Discuss opportunities to improve based on stories.

❑ On all site visits, reinforce your values. Don't be tolerant of anything that threatens them.

❑ How could you be Keeper of the Karma for your organization?

• _____

• _____

Practice 30

Promote Leadership at All Levels

Sue recently needed to get the air conditioning in her car fixed:

> *I called the dealer, who told me that it'd be three weeks before I could get an appointment and even then I'd have to bring in the car between eight and four. Frustrated, I decided to try my local Chevron station, having always found them to be friendly and helpful. "Is there anyone here who can fix my air conditioning during the evening or weekend?" I asked. "Or is that against some law?"*
>
> *"We can fix it whenever you want," said the attendant. "How about right now?"*
>
> *"Well, I need to go to a meeting about twenty miles away."*
>
> *"No problem. I'll drive you to your appoint-*

ment and pick you up afterward—your car should be ready by then."

I was a little blown away by the whole experience, but happy to get the problem taken care of.

When the young man came back to pick me up, I asked, "How can you afford to do service like this for your customers?"

"How can I afford not to?" he replied. "My name is Caesar. Didn't you know when you drove into my Chevron station that you were driving into Caesar's Palace?"

I found out when we got back to my car that Caesar doesn't own the station. He's a part-time worker who runs the place like he owns it.

A few months later, speaking to a group from Chevron Corporation, I mentioned my incredible experience. An executive told me that Caesar's Palace does three times the sales of any Chevron station in Northern California.

Many large organizations have a fatal flaw—their size works against them when changing direction. Companies like Intel, however, move at the speed of a sole proprietor. Intel broadcasts the executive vision directly to the individual level, then empowers employees to make their own decisions. "Most big organizations rely on one leader to make a decision and then wait for that decision to trickle down," says Jim Zurn. "Those organizations are like an aircraft carrier. You turn the wheel and it sort of turns . . . real . . . slow. We're more like a school of fish. A school might have tens of thousands of fish in it, but they can change together, instantaneously, and go in a new direction."

Give your people the tools and support they need and trust them to lead themselves. Then step up to become a visionary, mentor, and role model. You'll discover people like Caesar at all levels of your organization—people who run the place like they own it.

POWER TO THE PEOPLE

Jerry Williams was one of the toughest undercover cops on staff at the Housing Authority in Oakland, California. He was renowned for his phenomenal number of arrests.

With that reputation, it still seems strange to Jerry that in 1992 he was selected to be the first local police officer to try a new approach called community policing. "I thought, 'What the heck is "community policing"? I only know about busting people and dragging them to jail.'"

Before sending him off to crime-ridden Lockwood and Coliseum Gardens as the only on-site police officer, Jerry's commanding officer gave clear instructions. "He told me to do everything I did before, except add one thing—establish a rapport with the community. Nice idea. But how was I supposed to do that?"

So here comes Jerry, a tough cop in a community that

hates tough cops. Both parties desperately needed a new perspective. Jerry got his while busy "community policing"—he stumbled upon a community empowerment class. Jerry came back often and learned, with the rest of the group, that everyone has the power and wisdom to change their lives for the better.

His experience as a police officer reinforced the notion. "Driving offenders off to jail, almost every one would say, 'You don't understand. I really am a good person.' I'd just dismiss the idea. 'Yeah, right. You're in the back of my police car because you're just a low-life punk.' But I started thinking that maybe they really did have some good in them. They didn't need me, some hard-ass officer, swooping down and dragging them off to jail to make them realize they needed to change. What they needed was someone to foster that goodness and health and give them a chance to be better on their own."

That revelation brought with it a wave of optimism. "I suddenly understood what community policing meant. I got the residents together and said, 'We are going to turn this development into a community. You know what the problems are and you can come up with solutions, so let's start talking. I'm here to serve you and help you with what you need to get done.'"

The very first problem everybody came up with was the insensitivity of the police officers. Drugs and murders were listed second! Trust and

> *Tell me, and I will forget. Show me, and I may not remember. Involve me, and I will understand.*
>
> —NATIVE AMERICAN PROVERB

partnership were a big deal, and that was something that Jerry could address.

Understanding that the people must lead, Jerry set out to build "rapport." He got out of his police car and walked around the neighborhood to bridge the physical gap between himself and the people he served. He talked to residents about last night's game and life in general—anything but police stuff. He kept candy in his car for the kids, knowing he could be a positive role model and get a little closer to their skeptical parents.

Jerry's fellow police officers called him "The Lollipop Cop" and "Officer Friendly," and asked him all the time if it was "Hug a Thug Day." "Even my commanders told me, 'Jerry, you are the professional. You must dictate to them.' Well, I don't work like that anymore. Nobody is going to come in here and change the community except for the people of the community. They're the ones who live here. They know the problems and they have lots of solutions. My role is to help carry those solutions out. Officers tend to forget the *serve* part of *serve and protect*. They feel they need to dictate when they really should be putting the power into the hands of the people."

Jerry's results? Not a single murder in four years. Every drug dealer gone. The community is healthier and more united than ever. Now when officers question Jerry, they are anxious to know how he does it.

Jerry the cop is no longer the enforcer he once was. He now provides backup for the real leaders—the people of his community. Jerry's leadership style unleashed the wisdom, common sense, and creativity the residents always had.

IN PEOPLE WE TRUST

"When you strip away all the excuses for not empowering people, one thing remains: a lack of trust," maintains Larry Sternberg, who built an empire at The Ritz-Carlton Tysons Corner by promoting leadership at all levels. "Either you feel that if you do not control these individuals with policies, rules, and inspections they are going to commit malfeasance or you do not trust that they have the necessary knowledge, experience, and information to make a high-quality decision. The new role of a leader is to provide individuals and teams with that knowledge, experience, and information, then trust in them to make good decisions."

Schwab's Peter McIntosh agrees and says it all boils down to fundamental optimism. "Without an optimistic leader, an organization won't achieve its maximum potential," he says. "I have thousands of people working for me. If I believe they can't do the job, what am I going to do? Replace them all? I've got to hope they can do it and give them all the help I can. Trust is so important, but leaders forget it. They'll talk about trust, but everything they do is sort of counter to it. They analyze everything because they don't believe it will come out right. They bring in outsiders because they think

> *A great leader creates an aura or an environment of psychological security in which people can take risks.*
>
> —LARRY STUPSKI,
> Vice Chairman,
> The Charles Schwab
> Corporation

their own people can't get it done. Or they create controls and rules for when people make a mistake. Basic optimism replaces all that. If you want big things, you've got to assume you'll get them. If you look at successful leaders, very implicit in a lot of their success is just basic, simple human optimism."

When leaders give their people the tools, freedom, and trust they need to lead themselves, people take care of business with all the passion and commitment of a CEO. Still, many leaders hesitate to let their people run the show. Larry Sternberg finds this more than a little amusing. "It's funny how, from any given perspective, incompetence begins just one level below where you are," he says with a smile.

INSIGHT TO ACTION

Insight 8: Lead with Care

Promote Leadership at all Levels

❏ Circle where you think your people would rate you on the "Optimism Barometer."

Optimism Barometer

> 5—Believes we can leap tall buildings.
> 4—Believes we can leap townhouses.
> 3—Believes we can leapfrog.
> 2—"Leap when I say leap."
> 1—"No leaping. You'll probably get hurt."

❏ Ask your team members to list two things they'd do better if they owned the place. Let them do it.

- _____

- _____

❏ "We'd get better results if my relationship with _____ was stronger." Invite them to lunch.

Practice 31

Renew Yourself and Everyone Wins

Roger came home after a big snowstorm to find the whole neighborhood sledding in front of his house:

My two children ran up to me, and my daughter, Devon, shrieked, "Dad, Dad! You've got to try our sled. It's soooo scary! It's straight ice—you can barely steer!"

I was in no mood to go sledding. "Can't you see I've got my good business clothes on? If I went sledding, I'd tear my pants."

My son, Blake, got my attention when he said with disappointment, "Dad, you're losing the kid in you!"

I grabbed the sled out of his hands and shouted, "Come on kids! I'll show you how to sled!"

They were right. It was almost solid ice and I

could barely keep control. I almost hit a tree and
narrowly avoided a mailbox, but it was one of the
best days of my life.
I was right, too. I tore my pants.

Do you find it difficult to balance your life, family, and career? Today's fast-moving business environment leaves many leaders burned out, and their lives, families, and organization suffer. Children remind us that life is for living and having fun. Leaders are no exception. Recapturing the vibrant spirit of childhood means losing some control to gain some excitement and inspiration.

Renewal can come from within, or from taking a fresh look at the world around you. It comes from inspirational mentors, long-ignored passions, and quiet retreat.

STEAL WITH YOUR EYES AND EARS

"The most difficult thing about leadership is that you are the one who constantly energizes everybody else," says Horst Schulze. "When you're at the top, and you need somebody to energize *you*, there's hardly anybody there."

During the time The Ritz-Carlton was pursuing the Malcolm-Baldrige Award, Horst realized there were inspiring people and ideas all around him. "I began thinking about my business philosophy and realized that I learned it when I was a kitchen apprentice in Europe forty

years ago. The executive chef was very strict about offering a quality product and impeccable service, and told us
exactly how to go about it, based on his apprentice training fifty years before mine. I still believe that ninety-year-
old philosophy to be true, but the ways to achieve it aren't
fixed. There is no one right way, so I open my eyes and
ears to any ideas—no matter who or where they come
from. Steal with your eyes and ears—don't ever think you
know it all."

Horst has a voracious appetite for new ideas. After hear-
ing Mary Kay Ash speak at a recent Service/Quality
Leadership Forum 2000, Horst sprinted for the phones and
got his general managers on a conference call. He read off
the long list of ideas he just heard and encouraged his
managers to implement them at their hotels.

WHAT I'M DOING ISN'T SO HARD

Leaders can be recharged by anyone, not just peers.
Whenever Bill Marriott feels burned out, he knows where
to turn. "John McDonald works in the dish room at our
O'Hare hotel. He is blind. He's been sorting dishes and silverware there for over twenty years. He gets up at four in
the morning and takes two buses to work. He never
misses a day. When I go to the O'Hare Marriott, I always
stop by to see John. That energizes me for about a month. I
figure if he can get up and sort silver every single day,
what I am doing isn't so hard."

DON'T WAIT—DO IT NOW

"I had a heart attack and bypass surgery four years ago," says Larry Stupski of Schwab. "I got renewed all right— God renewed me. He kicked me off my old path and put me on a new one. Not a method I recommend." Larry now champions opportunities for Schwab employees to live a more balanced life.

John O'Neil says Larry's experience is a common one. John's extensive one-on-one work with religious, political, and business leaders reveals that most leaders only seek change when they hit rock bottom. "Hopefully, we can reverse that trend so that you don't wait until the heart attack to eat right and exercise. You don't wait until your spouse walks out the door to have a relationship with your family. The worst thing to do is delay change until something serious happens, because then you *have* to change. Constant renewal, constant retreat, and constant time-out is critical."

EASY RIDER

Mark Scott's relentless dedication to his hospital and community demands that he take time out for personal renewal. "All leaders work themselves to a frazzle," he says. "There's a point at which you're no longer true to yourself, your values, your family, or your organization. Everyone just has to get away. Let it rest, let yourself rest, let your organization rest. Renew your vision, your commitment, and your ability to think."

Every few years, Mark says good-bye to work and family and indulges his secret passion—taking off on his Harley-Davidson. He travels the country for a few months, taking in the sights and learning new skills. This year he learned to sail in Annapolis, then rode through the Shenandoah River Valley, up the St. Lawrence Seaway to Montreal, and down to Nashville. "Every day was so radically different than the days I'm used to—refreshing, exhilarating, and intoxicating." People at Mid-Columbia say when Mark returns from a trip, watch out—he's ready to roll at full throttle.

> *You can't do anything about the length of your life, but you can do something about its width and its depth.*
> —EVAN ESAR

Everyone has a passion that brought happiness and respite long ago, but nobody can find the time anymore. Sound familiar? Find the time. Your body, mind, family, and organization implore you.

LOOKING FOR LESSONS IN ALL THE WRONG PLACES

Carl Sewell searches everywhere for opportunities to learn and grow. He built six of the most successful automobile dealerships in North America by talking extensively with people who know nothing whatsoever about cars. Out-of-the-box thinking and an insatiable hunger for learning keep Carl going strong day after day.

Carl's cites his favorite piece of research—a University of Texas study that looked at over one hundred leaders from all sectors to find out what formative experiences or personal traits made them great. The study found only one factor that was present for every single leader—during their development, each spent quality time with other successful leaders. These results only strengthen Carl Sewell's dedication to seeking new perspectives.

When Carl first took over his father's fairly successful dealerships, he sought the wisdom of Stanley Marcus, founder of Neiman-Marcus. Stanley pointed out that Carl couldn't afford to hire him as a consultant. Undaunted, Carl asked if they could at least eat lunch together. Every month for the last eighteen years, Carl Sewell and Stanley Marcus have met for lunch to talk about business and life—anything and everything from excellence in service to whether or not weightlifting reverses the aging process. "Even after all these years," says Carl, "Stanley Marcus still teaches me how to live."

Carl seeks mentors wherever he can find them. "Len Schlesinger from Harvard taught me about the value of

> *You've got to be committed to lifelong learning, lifelong challenge, and lifelong renewal. You've got to repot yourself every once in a while.*
>
> —DAVID POTTRUCK,
> President and COO,
> The Charles Schwab
> Corporation

great measurement systems," he says. "Jack Welch from GE inspired me to focus on strategy implementation. Tom Peters reminded me of the power of people and customers. Tom Malone from Milliken showed me the power of recognition." Carl sees the world through as many eyes as possible. Peers, employees, customers, competitors, and even businesses that have nothing to do with cars are all considered important resources to learn from.

Carl believes leaders are not the only ones who need renewal: organizations benefit as well. "Learning and renewing must be built into our lives *and* our organizations," he says. Sewell dealerships are learning organizations with opportunities for growth and fresh perspectives at every level. Managers are rotated from dealership to dealership so that they gain a broader perspective of the business.

Carl's constant quest for knowledge, inspiration, and self-improvement gives both him and his organization an edge on the competition.

Carl Sewell meets with other great leaders to discuss life and business. Mark Scott takes off on his Harley. Bill Marriott talks with John, the blind silverware sorter. Learning, growing, and changing is a necessity for anyone, especially leaders. As John O'Neil says, "We live our lives so tightly wound, our souls can't breathe. To retreat is to let our souls breathe."

INSIGHT TO ACTION

Insight 8: Lead with Care

Renew Yourself and Everyone Wins

❑ Clear your calendar for "you." Each month, cancel five to ten appointments. Do something fun instead.

❑ List three things you'd love to do and do them more often.

- _____

- _____

- _____

❑ Who outside your business could mentor you? Get to know them.

Insight 8: Lead with Care

Practice 32

You Must Care

People don't care about how much you know until you show how much you care.

—KATHY HELOU,
National Sales Director,
Mary Kay Cosmetics

Kathy Helou remembers her first Mary Kay training class vividly. Her director asked, "If I could wave a magic wand over your head and make your dreams come true, where would you like to go in this company? Write it down on a piece of paper." Kathy, then twenty-eight years old, remembers writing down "pink Cadillac." But she was really thinking, "I'd rather be a national sales director. I don't know how I'll ever do it, but that's my goal." She recalls telling her husband that very night, "I'm going to be a national sales director by the time I'm forty."

Three months after her fortieth birthday, Kathy and an excited crowd of well-wishers squeezed into the small office in her home. She'd been tracking her sales numbers for the last few months, and that morning's orders put her over the top for the national sales director position. The phone rang, cutting through the noisy chatter. Shrieks of excitement turned to hushed whispers as Kathy, teary-eyed, picked up the phone. "Kathy, this is Gary Jinks from Mary Kay. Congratulations. You made it."

Kathy's achievement is amazing—but so is the fact that the phone call came *exactly when it was supposed to*. In most organizations sales results take weeks to be printed up, let alone trigger a phone call.

We couldn't wait to ask Larry Harley, president of Mary Kay Cosmetics, about the systems that make things run so efficiently. His response was powerful and unexpected.

"We don't need systems because we care. People here know Kathy and were rooting for her and wanting her to do well. They were looking for the order that put her over the top. As soon as they saw it, those people ran into Gary Jinks's office yelling, 'Kathy made it!' Gary made the call right away. That's why the call comes. Not because our systems are so good. Not because I'm so good. It's because people all through this organization care about each other."

PUT CARING AT THE TOP OF YOUR LIST

Complicated systems are not always the answer. Caring costs much less, and people like it much more. Mary Kay Ash learned long ago how caring can make a difference:

As a sales representative for Stanley Home Products, I went to hear the vice president of the company speak. He made a tremendous speech, and I wanted to tell him how moved I was by his words. It turned out there were a lot of people who felt the same, and I stood in line for a very long time. When I finally reached him, he shook hands with me, but he was looking over my shoulder to see how many more people were in line.

I was devastated. I really felt the man was wonderful and wanted to tell him so, but he didn't even hear what I had to say. I promised myself then and there, "If I ever get to be the person who's shaking the hands, I'm going to give my full attention to the person in front of me and never look to see how many more are in line." Because when you are talking to somebody, the only important person at that moment is the person right in front of you.

I was in Key West teaching some policemen about community policing, and one guy scoffed, "What do you want us to do? Hug 'em then cuff 'em?" I said, "No, that's kind of stupid. If you're going to arrest somebody, you cuff 'em then hug 'em."

—JERRY WILLIAMS,
Oakland, California
Community Police
Officer

Mary Kay has never broken the promise she made. Speaking with her, you feel her eyes lock onto your heart as if you are the only person in the room. She cares.

Customers also appreciate an organization that cares about its people. When you walk into a place of business, you know right away whether or not the employees are cared for and treated with respect. Your people and customers can sense sincerity—and the lack of it—a mile away.

Each of us becomes more dedicated and works harder when we are cared for and treated like human beings. Yet in life, and especially in business, we are too frugal when it comes to showing people we care. In business school and on the job we learn all about strategy implementation, planning techniques, how to read financials, and other such "matters of consequence." But at its core, business is about people.

LEADERSHIP AT ITS ESSENCE

One man provided great inspiration for this book. General Melvin Zais, 1916–1972, was a decorated general in World War II and Vietnam. Late in his life he spoke to the cadets of the Armed Forces War College. A tape of his speech landed in our hands years ago. His words epitomize the passion and commitment of a Turned On organization. General Zais speaks of leadership at its essence, and we are proud to close with his wisdom:

> *I would like to offer you one piece of advice that I believe will contribute more to making you a better leader and commander, will provide you with greater happiness and self-esteem, and at the same time advance your career more than any other advice which I can provide to you. And it doesn't call for a special personality, and it doesn't call for any certain chemistry. Any one of you can do it. And that advice is that you must care.*

You'll find that at this school, and any other service school that you might attend, beginning at your basic course, and winding up at war college level, that you spend about 80 percent of your time on tactics, strategy, weapons, planning, and writing—and you spend about 20 percent of your time on people matters. It's an interesting phenomenon, and a paradox, that after school we go to our units and what do we do? We spend about 80 percent of our time on people matters and about 20 percent of our time on tactics, weapons, logistics, and so forth. Everything you do has to do with people, and you must care about your soldiers and your sailors and your airmen.

Now, all of you are saying to yourself right now, "I care. What's this guy talking about?" Well, there are degrees of caring. And there are degrees of personal sacrifice to reflect the amount of caring that you do. And there's an attitude that you have to develop in yourself.

How do you know if you care? You're sitting out there wondering, "Do I care? Do I really care?" How do you know if you care?

Well, for one thing, you care if you really wonder what your soldiers do on their off-duty activities. When you're about to tee off on Saturday afternoon, when you're at the club at happy hour, or when you're going to church on Sunday, if you're wondering . . . if there's a little creeping nagging in the back of your head about, "I wonder what the soldiers are doing. I wonder." Do you do that? "What are the airmen doing? What are the sailors doing? Where do they go?" Then you care.

You care if you go in the mess hall—and I don't mean go

in with white gloves and rub dishes and pots and pans to find dust. You care if you go in the mess hall and notice that the scrambled eggs are in a big puddle of water and that twenty pounds of toast has been done in advance and it's lying there hard and cold. And bacon is lying there dripping in the grease. And the cooks got all their work done way ahead of time. And the cold pots of coffee are sitting on the table, getting even colder. If that really bothers you, if that really gripes you and you want to tear up those cooks, then you care.

When you are getting ready for the annual GI inspection, and you know your guys are working in the barracks. And you know they're working like hell and it's Sunday night. If you'll get out of your warm house and go down to the barracks to see them work and just sit on a foot locker. You don't have to tell them they're doing a great job. Just sit on a foot locker and talk to one or two soldiers and leave. They'll know that you know that they're working like hell to make you look good.

If you look out your window before a parade and you see that the troops are lined up there fifteen, twenty, thirty minutes before in windy, rainy, or hot weather, whatever it may be. If it doesn't really burn you to see that, you don't care. But if it does, you care. Because the only reason, the only reason that soldiers stand around and wait, is because some dumb jerk officer didn't plan it right, or he planned it in such a way that the troops had to pay for him not missing a deadline.

I can't make you do this. But you really, really need to like soldiers. You need to be amused at their humor. You

277

need to be tolerant of their bawdiness. You need to under-stand that they're as lousy as you let them be, and as good as you make them be. You just have to really like them, and feel good about being with them.

You cannot expect a soldier to be a proud soldier if you humiliate him. You cannot expect him to be brave if you abuse and cower him. You cannot expect him to be strong if you break him. You cannot ask for respect and obedience and willingness to assault hot landing zones and destroy dug-in emplacements if your soldier has not been treated with the respect and dignity which fosters unity, freedom, and personal pride.

The line between firmness and harshness, between strong leadership and bullying, between discipline and chicken, is a fine line. It is difficult to define. But those of us who are professionals—who have also accepted a career as leaders of men—must find that line. It is because judgment and con-cern for people and human relations are involved in leader-ship. Only men can lead, and not computers. I enjoin you to be ever alert to the pitfalls of too much authority. Beware that you do not fall into the category of the little man, with a little job, with a big head. In essence, be considerate. Treat your subordinates right and they will literally die for you.

Now, I want to close by stating that I realize that this was supposed to be a talk on the art of command. I didn't give you any high-level great secrets. I can't really tell you exactly how to be a great commander. But I want to say this. I want to say that if you care, I guarantee you a suc-cessful career. I won't guarantee that you will be a general or an admiral. If you do not become a flag officer, you will be happy in the devotion, love, and affection of your men, and you will like yourself better. I sincerely believe that to be a successful leader, in the idealistic sense, you must care. Thank you.

Vitality Scorecard

Use this tool to assess the balance of your organization and prioritize your action plan.

Instructions: Fill in the number that best describes how well your organization performs on each practice.

1. **POOR**—Doing very poorly, if at all.

2. **FAIR**—Doing a little, but have a long way to go.

3. **GOOD**—Doing well, but don't always execute fully.

4. **STRONG**—Doing extremely well, but not quite ready for benchmarking.

5. **BEST IN CLASS**—Others could benchmark us.

Insight 1: Build a Strong Foundation

1. Everyone knows the true essence of our business, and that clarity guides our every decision. (p. 6) _____

2. We intimately know our top customers and what's most important to them. (p. 13) _____

3. We design work based on how it is experienced by and affects our customers. (p. 21) _____

4. Our mission is clear, simple, and known by everyone. It inspires and guides people's actions because it is lived and felt by all. (p. 27) _____

5. We strongly emphasize the basics that matter most to our customers. This emphasis is never diminished by the pursuit of the latest technology or the next value-added idea. (p. 35) _____

INSIGHT 1 SUBTOTAL: _____

Insight 2: Make Every Customer Feel Special

1. We provide our customers with many product and service options that are based on their needs. (p. 45) _____

2. We consider each of our customers a segment of one. We tailor products and services to individuals. (p. 51) _____

3. We have the freedom and tools to treat each of our customers like a close friend or family member. We are known by our customers as the company that has real people who truly care. (p. 57) _____

INSIGHT 2 SUBTOTAL: _____

Insight 3: Have the Courage to Set Bold Goals

1. We excel at our short-term objectives while simultaneously and ruthlessly inventing a new future. (p. 71) _____

2. We aggressively pursue new perspectives, encouraging everyone to take risks and discover new solutions. (p. 80) _____

3. We continually forge partnerships with customers, suppliers—even competitors—for our mutual benefit. (p. 88) _____

INSIGHT 3 SUBTOTAL: _____

Insight 4: Simplify, Simplify, Simplify

1. Every person can name the three goals the organization aims for and has clear, personal objectives to help hit those targets. (p. 98) _____

2. Every process and system is designed to cost-effectively give customers what they want and simplify their experience. (p. 104) _____

3. We outlaw all unnecessary meetings, memos, rules, and regulations to free people to work creatively and efficiently. When a memo arrives on my desk, I know that it must be very important. (p. 110) _____

INSIGHT 4 SUBTOTAL: _____

Insight 5: Make Technology Your Servant

1. We use technology to provide our customers with direct access to the heart of our business—when and how they want it. (p. 125) _____

2. We invest in and exploit technology to the fullest to capitalize on every encounter with a customer. We capture feedback, immediately act on problems, and use that information to create stronger relationships and better ways of doing business. (p. 133) _____

3. Technology is designed hand-in-hand with our people and customers, resulting in incredibly effective and efficient systems. (p. 140) _____

INSIGHT 5 SUBTOTAL: _____

Insight 6: Measure Well, Act Fast

1. We look at the dollar impact of every customer problem before we make decisions or invest money. When we do spend money, we get the best return on our investment. (p. 155) _____

2. The customer feedback we measure is representative of reality and leads us to the right decisions. (p. 161) _____

3. We only measure a few critical areas that are relevant and based on our priorities. Our mea-

sures ensure a balanced focus on what's most important for people, customers, and profits. (p. 168) _____

4. Our measurements are not gathering dust. We immediately act to improve results. (p. 173) _____

INSIGHT 6 SUBTOTAL: _____

Insight 7: Unleash the Power of People

1. Our hiring program ensures that we only bring on board people who live our values and match the profile of our best performers. They not only have the capability, but the heart and initiative to succeed. (p. 185) _____

2. Our people love coming to work—they are challenged, stimulated, and supported. They are clear on their role and contribution. (p. 192) _____

3. Teamwork is essential here—communication, connection, and focus are constant. (p. 199) _____

4. Learning doesn't just happen en masse at orientations or annual training courses. It is constant and tailored to individual needs. (p. 208) _____

5. Our compensation program is in exact alignment with our top priorities. People know where they can make the greatest contribution and are paid to make it. (p. 217) _____

6. Every person feels appreciated and knows that someone will notice when they do a great job. Personal recognition is constant and heartfelt. (p. 225)   _____

7. We encourage and celebrate the amazing individuals who make a difference every day. (p. 234)   _____

INSIGHT 7 SUBTOTAL: _____

Insight 8: Lead with Care

1. Senior management and top leaders are the embodiment of their values. They live and practice what they preach. Everyone knows exactly what the leaders care about most. (p. 248)   _____

2. We grow leaders on all levels so that we can quickly and efficiently make decisions and take action. (p. 256)   _____

3. Everyone is encouraged to live a balanced life and refresh the mind, body, and spirit through regular renewal. (p. 264)   _____

4. There is an honest feeling of mutual trust and caring for each other here. (p. 272)   _____

INSIGHT 8 SUBTOTAL: _____

CHART YOUR ORGANIZATION'S VITALITY

	Insight Subtotal		Insight Score

Insight 1:
Build a Strong Foundation: _____ ÷ 5 = _____

Insight 2:
Make Every Customer Feel Special: _____ ÷ 3 = _____

Insight 3:
Have the Courage to Set Bold Goals: _____ ÷ 3 = _____

Insight 4:
Simplify, Simplify, Simplify: _____ ÷ 3 = _____

Insight 5:
Make Technology Your Servant: _____ ÷ 3 = _____

Insight 6:
Measure Well, Act Fast: _____ ÷ 4 = _____

Insight 7:
Unleash the Power of People: _____ ÷ 7 = _____

Insight 8:
Lead with Care: _____ ÷ 4 = _____

TOTAL (out of 40 possible points): _____

1. Complete the Vitality Scorecard yourself.

2. Ask your people to complete the Vitality Scorecard. Is there a difference in your perceptions? Discuss the reasons why.

3. Prioritize your actions. Which two Insights need the most attention?

   • _____

   • _____

4. On which questions did you score a 1 or a 2? Go to the page number listed after those questions and review the stories, ideas, and exercises presented.

Acknowledgments

Our book would still be a "work in progress" without the total involvement and commitment of Jenny Lasser. She spent a year capturing people's stories in their own words, always remaining true to their passion. She painstakingly researched and double-checked everything. She truly lived with the book, crafting words, paragraphs, and chapters with a "good enough never is" attitude.

Working side by side with Jenny, Sam Zeszut brought his creative flair to everything from subtitles to phrasing. Just when we thought we had it right, Sam would say, "Have you thought about this . . ." Jenny and Sam brought a great deal of energy, talent, and heart to the project, and we're very thankful to have them on the team.

We want to thank our agent, Jonathon Lazear, for believing in the viability of the project, introducing us to our publisher, HarperCollins, and guiding us along the way. HarperBusiness's publishing director, Adrian Zackheim, would always infuse us with confidence with his words, "We love the book—don't worry, it's going to be terrific." Our editor at HarperBusiness, Kirsten Sandberg, was a wonderful mentor, friend, and coach—and she taught us a tremendous amount about the English language along the way. Lisa Berkowitz, Harper's director of marketing communications, is the best in the business, and we sincerely appreciate the enthusiasm she brought to the project from day one.

Looking back, our thoughts, ideas, and inspiration for the book can be traced to four people who have influenced us greatly over the years. To Bill Marriott, Bob Noyce, Tom Peters, and Tom Malone, we want to say thank you, and we are thrilled that our paths crossed.

Our appreciation to Karen Beckwith for all of her organization and for always finding a way to get the impossible done. We want to thank Stacie Canova for all of the evenings and weekends she spent transcribing our volumes of interviews. Thanks to Steve Clarke for his ability to turn a stack of typewritten pages into an interesting and engaging layout.

We all know how important it is to get feedback from those you respect. Several good friends and colleagues became even better friends through their willingness to read our initial drafts and give us their valued input. Thank you: Rick Barlow, Ann Bowers, Brian Dietmeyer, Owais Durrani, Charles Garfield, Ken Luchansky, John Mathewson, John O'Neil, Robin Diane Orr, Georganne Papac, Mike Pusateri, and Sam Shriver.

The encouragement to write this book came from the Service/Quality Leadership Forum 2000 advisory board, who have become good friends and have guided us along the way. Thank you: Bill Cooney, Tom Davis, John Goodman, Robin Diane Orr, Horst Schulze, and Carl Sewell.

Our Insights were inspired by spending time with the members of the Service/Quality Leadership Forum 2000.

We appreciate their candid input and their allowing us to go behind the scenes of their great organizations: ADP Claims Solutions Group; AGA: Allied Graphic Arts; AT&T; Ascent Entertainment Group; Baxter Healthcare; Blue Cross/Blue Shield of New Jersey; British Airways; Compaq; California School of Professional Psychology; Community Health Realization Institute; Datatec Industries; C.R. England & Sons; The Freeman Companies; Garden Ridge Pottery; The Healthcare Forum; Herman Miller; Hewlett-Packard; Holiday Rambler; Holt Companies; Indigo America; Intel; Levi Strauss & Co.; Pitney Bowes Software; Mannington Resilient Floors; Marriott International; Mary Kay Cosmetics; Merck; Mid-Columbia Medical Center; Miller SQA; Milliken & Co.; Motorola; Niagara Mohawk Power Corp.; Nissan Motor Company; Oracle Federal; The Robin Orr Group; Pepsi-Cola Company; Pitney Bowes Credit Corporation; RE/MAX International; The Ritz-Carlton Hotel Company; Rosenbluth Travel; Rural/Metro Corporation; Charles Schwab & Co.; SEMATECH; Sewell Motor Company; TARP; Texas A&M University; Think Customer; *USA Today*; USAA; Weisman Enterprises; Williams-Sonoma; and Xerox Corporation.

Our special thanks to all of the individuals who shared their stories with us and provided the foundation and support for our work: Eli Anders, Mary Kay Ash, Lindy Ashmore, Craig Barrett, Bill Baughman, Bill Blanchard, Gerhard Blendstrup, Jim Bolin, Miller Bonner, Liam Bradshaw, John Seely Brown, Joan Brunner, Stephanie Butler, Chris Carey, Randy Carter, Tom Chase, Chip Chipman, Dell Chisolm, John Coghlan, Russ Coile, Kent

Colwell, Bill Cooney, Yollanda Copeland, Zach Craycroft, Dave Crowley, Arthur Coulombe, Joyce Davis, Jan De Puy, Blake and Devon Dow, Keith Erickson, Jake Farmer, Steven Freund, John Gaulding, Bill Gerard, Pete Glass, Abby Gonzalez, John Goodman, Barbara Gross, Jodi Harley, Larry Harley, Kathy Hausman, Kathy Helou, Michele Hunt, Kate James, Wendy Jarvis, Vivian Jefferson, Barney Johnson, John Karolzak, Rick Karp, Tom Kasten, Sue Kelly, Gina King, Craig Lambert, Lynne Lancaster, Arlene Lenarz, Eleanor Lopez, Cynthia Lowe, Susanne Lyons, Tom Malone, Bob Manschot, Bill Marriott Jr., Kathy Marshall, Marvin Martinez, Judith McCrackin, Mick McGill, Steve McGuire, Peter McIntosh, Regis McKenna, Thomas McKeon, Pat Mene, Anita Miller, Roger Mills, Marie Minarich, Emily Morgan, Don Murphy, Larry Murphy, Kathy O'Brian, John O'Neil, Robin Orr, Carlos Permell, Tom Peters, Michelle Pitter-Jones, Ron Pobuda, David Pottruck, Karen Prazak, Steven Rauscher, Bob Rockey, Carter Russel, Marsha Scarbrough, Horst Schulze, Chuck Schwab, Jacque Scott, Mark Scott, Judy Sedgeman, Tom Seip, Don Seta, Carl Sewell, Rhonda Shasteen, Albert "Smitty" Smith, Andy Sorensen, Michele Spatz, Bill Spencer, Greg Spirakis, Frank Steenberg, Larry Sternberg, Larry Stupski, Brent Threadgill, Tim Timmerman, Cheryl Valdez, Gary VanSpronsen, Atul Vashistha, Wendy Watson, Jann Westfal, Heidi Wetterberg, Jim Whittaker, Brian Williams, Jerry Williams, Beverley Wilson, Kathy Winkleman, Allison Woods, Vicki Young, and Jim Zurn.

292

Index